W9-CMD-768

THE HAMMARSKJÖLD FORUMS

Case Studies
on
The Role of Law
in the
Settlement of International Disputes

DISARMAMENT

BACKGROUND PAPERS AND PROCEEDINGS
of
THE FOURTH HAMMARSKJÖLD FORUM

LOUIS HENKIN
Author of the Working Paper

LYMAN M. TONDEL, Jr.
Editor

Published for
THE ASSOCIATION OF THE BAR OF THE CITY OF NEW YORK
by
OCEANA PUBLICATIONS, INC.
DOBBS FERRY, N.Y.
1964

CARNEGIE LIBRARY
LIVINGSTONE COLLEGE
SALISBURY, N. C. 28144

(C) 1964 by

THE ASSOCIATION OF THE BAR OF THE CITY OF NEW YORK

All Rights Reserved

Library of Congress Catalog Card Number: 63-19588

PRINTED IN THE UNITED STATES OF AMERICA

341.67
H224

Table of Contents

Participants   VII
Editor's Foreword   IX

Part One

THE WORKING PAPER

Disarmament—The Lawyer's Interests, *by* Louis Henkin   1

Introduction   1

I. Disarmament in Post-War International Politics   3

   A. Disarmament and Arms Control: Definitions   3

   B. Armaments and International Relations   5

   C. The Foreign Policies of East and West   7

   D. Armament in East-West Policies   9

   E. Disarmament in East-West Policies   11

   F. Seventeen Years of Failure   13

   G. Why Nations Have Not Disarmed   16

   H. The Prospects   19
      1. Today's Weapons and Their Uses
      2. The Modest Promises of Disarmament
      3. Political Change and Disarmament Prospects

   I. Disarmament and the Other Nations   26

II. The Special Concerns of the Lawyer   27

   A. Armaments and International Law   28

   B. Disarmament Agreements and Their Enforcement   28
      1. Inducing Nations to Observe Disarmament
         Agreements
      2. If a Violation Occurs
      3. Verification and Inspection
      4. Organization of Inspection Systems
      5. Responses

   C. Maintaining the Peace in a Disarming World   35

   D. Disarmament and United States Law   37

III. The Lawyer in the Community   40

91333

Part Two

A SUMMARY OF THE FORUM PROCEEDINGS

Participants: Arthur H. Dean, John N. Hazard, Louis Henkin and John T. McNaughton

I.	Disarmament: Context and Prospect	45
	A. Seventeen Years of Failure	45
	B. The Modest Promises of Disarmament	47
II.	The Military Context	50
	A. The Role of the Unilateral Decision	52
III.	The Soviet Union: Objectives and Means	53
IV.	The Role of the United States	56
	A. The Postwar Setting	56
	B. Disarmament Proposals	57
V.	Disarmament and Other Nations	63
VI.	The Lawyer's Role	65

APPENDICES

A.	Highlights of Disarmament Efforts, 1945-1963, A Chronology	69
B.	Text of Treaty Banning Nuclear Weapon Tests in the Atmosphere, in Outer Space and under Water signed at Moscow on August 5, 1963	75

SELECTED BIBLIOGRAPHY	79
NOTES TO THE WORKING PAPER	95

THE FOURTH HAMMARSKJÖLD FORUM

April 29, 1963

Participants

THE HONORABLE ARTHUR H. DEAN
Chairman, United States Delegation to the 18-Nation
Disarmament Conference, 1962

JOHN N. HAZARD
Professor of Public Law, Columbia University

LOUIS HENKIN
Hamilton Fish Professor of International Law and Diplomacy
and Professor of Law, Columbia University

THE HONORABLE JOHN T. MCNAUGHTON
General Counsel, Department of Defense

EDITOR'S FOREWORD

In 1960-61 The Association of the Bar of the City of New York was forcefully reminded by two of its senior members, James N. Rosenberg and Grenville Clark, that it should be devoting more of its resources and attention to the cause of world peace through law. It was not that it had by any means defaulted in this field of law, but rather that none of its existing committees or activities was intended to concentrate on the primary challenge to lawyers in our day—namely, the role of law in the settlement of international disputes.

After exploring numerous possibilities it was concluded to conduct, as forums, a series of case studies. It was deliberately decided to consider disputes of the first magnitude, involving political, military, economic and social, as well as legal, problems. It was understood that existing law might be found to play a minor role in these controversies. Yet it was felt that the role of law, whatever it might be, should be more fully appreciated because if there is to be meaningful progress towards international arms control or disarmament and the elimination of war as a means of settling international disputes, then means of settlement alternate to war—means under law—must be developed.

It was recognized that under the spur of ever more devastating weapons, there have been in the last 70 years a series of significant steps in the development of peaceful means for settling international controversies—including the Hague Conventions; the League of Nations and the Permanent Court of International Justice; the United Nations and the International Court of Justice; the Organization of American States; and the Court of Justice of the European Economic Community. These steps have not, however, prevented war. In this sense they have all failed.

Yet, in a larger sense, these efforts may not have failed. World law may be impractical, or impossible of achievement at this stage of human history, but these steps and others may have marked the way towards some of the elements of a world at peace under law. They certainly have reflected, and helped induce, a far more extensive consideration of the problems of peacefully settling inter-

IX

national disputes than ever before. And they have had results that should be more generally known. For example, in only one adversary case decided by the Permanent Court of International Justice or the International Court of Justice has the losing nation failed to abide by the Court's decision; and all of the rulings of the Court of Justice of the European Economic Community, many of which have involved economic matters of major concern to the disputants, have been carried out. The United Nations has prevented wars. There has, through all this, been a sort of common law development of the means of peaceful settlement of international disputes even though wars and rumors of war still fill the air.

Accordingly it was concluded that it might be useful, and should surely be educational, for there to be a series of case studies in the role of law in settling international disputes, and three forums were held in 1962, and two in 1963, all at the House of the Association in New York City. A sixth is in the planning stage as this is written. The first considered the Berlin-German crisis; the second, the United Nations action in the Congo; the third, the Cuban crisis of October, 1962; the fourth, Disarmament; and the fifth, the international position of Communist China. A volume in this series has been prepared for each of the first four of these subjects. Each volume contains (1) an outstanding Working Paper, prepared by a prominent legal scholar in the field, which summarizes, but with appropriate detail, the legal and factual background of the dispute; (2) a condensation of the discussion at the Forum by the author of the Working Paper and commentators who included leading experts in the affairs discussed; and (3) an extensive bibliography prepared by the Research Staff of the Association's Library. Due to the unique access of the Association to the United Nations, to national leaders, and to prominent legal scholars, the participants have been notable.

As previously indicated, it was recognized in planning this series that such major disputes as those in Berlin, the Congo and Cuba, that regarding disarmament and arms control, and that regarding China could not, in practice, be solved exclusively under existing legal methods and that, in any event, rights and duties under law comprised only part of the problem in each case. Yet it clearly appeared at the Forums that the nations involved did have legal rights and duties; that even the Soviet Union seeks to justify, and with great particularity, its actions in the name of law and, for all we know, may have rejected some courses of action for which even their apologists could not rationalize any legal justification; that rules, or at least patterns, of conduct by nations, by groups of nations, and by the United Nations, are being constantly developed, as in the Congo and in the Inter-American system; and that the experience being acquired in peacefully trying to solve these disputes must be understood if progress is to be made.

If, as we must hope, fear of nuclear devastation is to drive the nations into finding means of peacefully solving controversies with each other, the search for such means can only be hastened by greater understanding of what actions, ambitions, needs or ideologies lead to critical disputes; of what procedures and devices have helped solve such disputes, and what have not; of what new law is evolving in connection with efforts to solve such disputes; of the extent to which rulers have had regard for at least the pretext of legality; and of what sanctions and obligations have restrained them the most.

In addition to inspiring this series of Forums, James N. Rosenberg of the New York Bar made a substantial financial contribution which enabled the Association to embark on the project. A grant was made by the Ford Foundation early in 1963 to enable the series to continue, and a portion of the earlier cost was met by a grant from the Ottinger Foundation, Inc.

As the original planning of this series neared completion, Dag Hammarskjöld, an honorary member of the Association, was tragically killed in the course of a mission of peace. As a memorial to him the series was entitled "The Hammarskjöld Forums." Adlai E. Stevenson, United States Permanent Representative to the United Nations, and his Deputy, Francis T. P. Plimpton, inaugurated the Forums at the first meeting which was devoted to a consideration of the Berlin-German crisis. Remarks made by them on that occasion are included in Volume I.

Before the second Forum, on April 30, 1962, on The Legal Aspects of the United Nations Action in the Congo, His Excellency U Thant, Acting Secretary-General of the United Nations, dedicated to Dag Hammarskjöld's memory The Hammarskjöld Room in the House of The Association of the Bar of the City of New York. His dedication is included in Volume II.

In publishing these volumes it is hoped by the Association that each will provide some of those who conduct public discussions, as well as some students and teachers, with background information on a specific controversy; that each will alert the reader to the existing and developing law involved in the particular controversy;

and that all who read may thereby become more aware that only by the substitution of the rule of law may war be eliminated as the ultimate means of settling international disputes.

Lyman M. Tondel, Jr.

PART ONE

THE WORKING PAPER

WORKING PAPER: DISARMAMENT—THE LAWYER'S INTERESTS

LOUIS HENKIN

Hamilton Fish Professor of International Law and Diplomacy and Professor of Law, Columbia University

INTRODUCTION

For seventeen years now the Government of the United States has been engaged in negotiation about disarmament. During that time, every leader in this nation, as in every nation, has proclaimed the terrible urgency of achieving disarmament of some kind in some measure. Continued failure has bred increasing hopelessness and skepticism; it has not weakened the protestations of governments as to the need for disarmament, nor kept any one of them from the negotiating table. In the United States, in and out of government, more thought is given to the problems of disarmament than ever before.

As in other areas of public life, lawyers have been prominent in the disarmament efforts of the United States Government. Most American disarmament negotiators have been lawyers; most of those in charge of the formulation of disarmament policy have been lawyers. But unlike other areas of national policy, the leadership of lawyers in the disarmament efforts of government has not been matched by a corresponding interest among lawyers in the community. The lawyer who speaks knowingly of the Congo and Berlin is not yet fluent about "second-strike capability" and "stabilized deterrence," his references to "inspection" are hardly knowledgeable or sophisticated. For this ignorance, and indifference, there are no longer good reasons. Despite security classifications and the complexity of military technology, the issues of armament and disarmament are now largely in the public domain. The drought in public disarmament literature of half-a-dozen years ago has given way to a flood of books, studies, articles, some of them clear, sophisticated and illuminating.

Disengagement from any public issue by any group of literate citizens is to be regretted. The lack of concern of lawyers—vocal

1

leaders of community opinion—with the problems of disarmament may prove especially unfortunate. National policy on disarmament may yet prove another field for battle; it may—again—require the dedicated efforts of the legal community to strive for reason and order in international relations. Doubts and fears about disarmament, in the community and in the Congress, threaten to restrain or retard Executive efforts to pursue the national interest along the path of agreed disarmament. The Legal Community may have to help assure fair hearing and fair consideration for disarmament proposals that might be negotiated.

The lawyer also has special, professional interests in disarmament. For the international lawyer the negotiation and drafting of any international agreement is, of course, a particular specialty. Agreement, if achieved, may also bring new international institutions to administer international disarmament. Agreement may require, too, new institutions for maintaining peace in a disarming world, new rules of international behavior, new procedures for settling disputes between nations.

There are also special concerns for the domestic lawyer. Any foreseeable disarmament agreement, it seems often forgotten, would have corresponding application within the United States. Agreement may make novel treaties, and novel implementing legislation, the law of our land, affecting the activities of government, the interests of industry and commerce, perhaps subjecting the rights and privacies of citizens to foreign scrutiny and inspection. It may bring economic dislocation requiring organized relocations and readjustments by legislative and administrative action.

These are the variated interests of the lawyer in the issues of disarmament—and, therefore, this Hammarskjöld forum. In introduction, this working paper will attempt to set forth in briefest compass the nature of the disarmament problem, and to suggest, in particular, those aspects of it that are of special concern to the lawyer. Hopefully, it will lead the reader to page 79, the bibliography.

I. DISARMAMENT IN POST-WAR INTERNATIONAL POLITICS

A. *Disarmament and Arms Control: Definitions*

Disarmament was once a simple term. Early international usage contemplated formal international agreement to eliminate or reduce armies and armaments. Today the definition is less simple. The principal complication, perhaps, is reflected in the concept of "arms control," to be distinguished from "disarmament." For this distinction, disarmament means the reduction or elimination of weapons and vehicles for delivering them, as well as prohibitions on their further manufacture; arms control, strictly, means that weapons will remain, but that nations may conclude agreements about their use or deployment in order to reduce the likelihood or the severity of war: *e.g.*, President Eisenhower's "Open Skies" proposal[1] to inform other nations how arms are being deployed, or provisions for "early warning" of possible attack,[2] or suggestions for direct White House-Kremlin telephones. (Others use arms control to describe, generally, a cooperative approach to armament policy between nations, which may also include some disarmament.) Proponents of comprehensive disarmament, including official spokesmen of the Soviet Union, have often dismissed arms control as the merest palliative, and have sometimes even condemned such controls as pretexts for espionage and military intelligence for hostile purposes. At best, critics might say, arms control may prevent war by accident or mistake, and may serve as some deterrent; it will not eliminate war because it does not eliminate the means of waging war.[3] Others have urged that in the present state of East-West relations only small steps are possible at first; controls to assure against surprise attack or accidental war may be more meaningful than small reductions in armaments, and will breed confidence necessary for true disarmament later. In fact, there are those who see the best hopes for international peace, and the only hopes for agreement, not in important reductions or eliminations of weapons, but in controls on existing weapons and in restrictions on future development.[4]

3

In negotiations today, distinction between disarmament and arms control does not pose a major issue. Both have been subjects of international negotiation. The Soviet Union continues to call for a ban on testing nuclear weapons, though that can hardly be called "disarmament." And the United States, frequently accused of seeking only arms control, has in fact made proposals for comprehensive disarmament involving substantial reductions in armaments and armies even in early stages.[5] It is only if disarmament is carried very far that it acquires a very different character. Early stages of disarmament, like arms control proposals, are possible national policies in a political context not unlike the one we know; anything approaching general and complete disarmament entails clearly a very different international order—as the comprehensive proposals of both the United States and the Soviet Union make clear. For our purposes, however, it will not contribute to clarity to deal separately with arms control and disarmament. The terms will be used interchangeably, to include any agreement to eliminate or reduce armies or armaments, to prohibit or limit their further production or development, to govern the possession, deployment or use of those that remain.

A different variant from traditional thinking about international disarmament involves the "tacit agreement."[6] Greater sophistication about international politics, about cold-wars and weapons-strategy, has led to recognition that nations in fact "agree" —act in concert or correspondingly—about their armaments without formal agreements, even without negotiation. When the United States and Canada refrain from arming their borders or deploying warships on the Great Lakes, they are in a kind of tacit agreement about their armaments. More significantly, if the Soviet Union should sharply reduce its forces, NATO might well "agree" by reacting correspondingly. And indeed, since a large rise in the military budget of the Soviet Union would undoubtedly lead to an increase in that of the United States, one may speak of a tacit agreement between the United States and the U.S.S.R. not to escalate unduly their respective military budgets. Observers may say that there has been, in effect, a tacit agreement between the United States and the U.S.S.R. not to give nuclear weapons to respective allies, whether China or France. Some see real hope for arms control only in unilateral action—*e.g.*, by adopting an arms program that is clearly for retaliation not for "first strike." Of course, "tacit agreements" differ from formal ones in important respects: one

4

is not always sure that they exist; it is easier to terminate them; and they may not long be complied with. But then, they do not have to be painfully negotiated, and usually they call for no complicated inspection to verify that they are being observed nor for other institutions to administer or enforce them. It may well be, as some believe, that additional tacit "agreements" can be planned and developed, and that these afford the most promising avenue for assuring peace, even for achieving some disarmament. In this paper, however, we deal primarily with the efforts of government to achieve disarmament by agreement.

B. *Armaments and International Relations*

One can only be amazed at the persistence of the attitude which reacts to disarmament as a discrete national policy separate from other military and foreign policies. There appears no greater obstacle to understanding than the failure to see disarmament today as an aspect of defense policy in a nation's total foreign policy.[7] Disarmament means no armaments, or less armaments, or controlled armaments. Disarmament can be acceptable only if it serves better, or as well, the purposes for which nations build and maintain armaments, or has other countervailing advantages to national interest. For years, the United States has believed that its national security, and other important national interests, required that it maintain tremendous national armaments. The critical question for the United States is whether agreement with other nations—in particular, with Russia—to disarm or to control armaments will contribute, better than free competition in armament, to peace, security, and other aims of our foreign policy.[8] The question can be broken down: Will the likelihood of terrible war be enhanced or reduced if there is some disarmament? Will the United States be more or less secure? Will our national interests be advanced or jeopardized, if instead of continuing the race with Russia we persuade her to reduce her armaments for corresponding reductions by us? To answer these questions, we may have to ask further: How will disarmament affect the Cold War? If the Cold War continues, will disarmament help or hinder the United States in its economic and political struggle with Communism? How will our disarmament affect other interests, foreign or domestic?

The answers to these questions are the quest of American

5

Disarmament policy. And the answers are not easy. Of course, they will depend in largest part on exactly what a "disarmament" agreement contains, but any substantial agreement can be assayed only by complex and imprecise estimates and guesses as to its consequences for national purposes, particularly those now served by our armaments. And since agreement involves other nations, any effort to understand the history of disarmament efforts, or to assess their prospects for the future, must ask similar questions about them—in particular, the Soviet Union. What are Soviet interests as they see them? How do armaments, how would disarmament, affect the realization of these interests?[9] For both the United States and the U.S.S.R., moreover, the exploration is complicated by the fact that armament and arms programs, like other national policies, do not respond neatly and logically to particular national needs. Arms programs and an international arms race, once begun, acquire impetus, motivations, reasons and rationalizations not clearly directed to primary national policies. Disarmament efforts have to take into account, too, those accretions that are not in the direct relation between armaments and national foreign policy. Of course, disarmament programs and negotiations may also acquire "reasons" which are not totally relevant to the impact of disarmament on national security or other national foreign policy.[10]

We speak, it will be noted, largely in terms of the United States and the Soviet Union. In theory, and in the long run, disarmament involves and must involve all the nations of the world with any military capacity or potential. But since the Second World War, the important armaments have been concentrated in the hands of the two giants and their allies. Disarmament negotiations have in fact been governed by the military power, potential, aspirations and fears of these two camps. It is they, principally, who have negotiated about disarmament. The disarmament about which they have negotiated consists primarily of limitations and controls on their own armaments. And the other nations, earnestly and repeatedly resolving and urging disarmament, have had in mind the disarmament of the super-powers, the elimination or control of their weapons of massive destruction, the slowing down, at least, of their arms race.

The emphasis here, then, is principally on "bi-polar" disarmament. That, too, we shall see has to take into account what several other nations might be prepared to do. General multi-

6

lateral disarmament, on the other hand, seems a subsequent and a largely separable question; unless there is first some bi-polar disarmament the disarmament of other nations seems remote and unlikely. The problems and prospects of such multilateral disarmament will be mentioned later, and briefly.

C. *The Foreign Policies of East and West*

One can hardly state, in a paragraph or a page, the principal goals and motivations of even our own foreign policy. To attempt it for the Soviet Union courts the additional dangers of ignorance and bias. But some recollection of the principal motivations of East and West is essential to a beginning of wisdom about disarmament.

A principal concern of every nation is the maintenance of national security. Surely, it was a principal motivation of Soviet policy after the Second World War, and the Soviet Union retained and augmented its armies and armaments partly for that purpose. Whether Russia was justified in feeling threatened, whether there was any basis for fear of future danger, may be immaterial. The United States, on the other hand, disarmed drastically after World War II, but it did have the Atomic Bomb. United States rearmament when it began was designed, immediately and directly, not to defend our own borders, but for the defense of others against the threat of Communist expansion. Of course, our own national interests and our own security were ultimately involved.

The heart of the foreign policies of East and West, and their need for armaments, lay in these conflicting policies. The story is familiar. The Soviet Union sought early opportunities to bring about friendly governments on its borders and to eliminate "forever" the threat of a resurgent Germany. Whether its early and successful post-war efforts to communize Eastern Europe were motivated by fears for its military security, or by an affirmative zeal for exporting Communism, is not beyond debate; perhaps both motives had important influence. In any event, the effort was brought to a halt by resistance, supported principally by the United States, in Iran, Greece and Turkey. Under United States leadership, the West responded to Soviet expansionism with a policy of "containment" which, over the years, comprised many policies: rearmament; NATO and lesser alliances; the war in

7

Korea; resistance to Communist forces in what was Indo-China; recently, actions and reactions in Cuba.

These were the confrontations involving directly military power. When United States power offset that of the Soviet Union to achieve a stalemate, the struggle did not cease; only its instruments changed. One may even describe, loosely, as Soviet "expansionism" and U.S. "containment," the conflict which constitutes the Cold War in its non-military aspects, the competition vis-à-vis other nations, old and especially new. One may describe in terms of expansionism Soviet support for radical movements for self-determination which it may hope to help transform into "people's revolutions," if necessary by subversion and various forms of inter-vention. One may describe as "containment" U.S. policy to thwart communism by supporting stability and encouraging peaceful change and development, with force in the wings ready to inter-vene to contain any communist effort to achieve change by violence and subversion.

To describe United States and Soviet policies in these terms, it should be added, may be to distort them. The United States, one may hope, pursues a foreign policy which is not merely a reaction to Communism. Affirmatively, the United States seeks its own peace and prosperity in a world in which other nations too would be free, in independence and diversity, to pursue their own aspirations in their own way. Describing U.S.-Soviet relations as we have is also deceptive in that it aggravates the stress on the "bi-polarity" of post-war international relations. Even at the height of the Cold War, "bi-polarity" might, at most, describe the foci of military power; politically, the concept was misleading. It conceal-ed that Soviet policy was offensive, that of the United States defensive; that Soviet policy was not aimed directly at the United States in the same sense that U.S. policy focused on Communist expansion: the U.S.S.R. sought to expand elsewhere, anywhere; the United States intervened to contain it where the danger lay. More recently, surely, the "bi-polar" character of the world, in political terms, has been much modified.[11] There are, of course, the fissures in each camp, even if De Gaulle's France and Com-munist China may represent very different political phenomena. Inevitably, these developments within each side will affect, in ways not yet discernible, the character of the confrontation between East and West. More significantly, perhaps, while East and West seem still mesmerized by each other, the new nations have achieved

8

status, not of a military third force, but of substantial political independence and even of important political influence in world affairs. (Their influence is, in fact, enhanced by the Cold War, which impels both sides to woo their favors.)

D. *Armament in East-West Policies*

The decreasing bi-polarity of international relations may, we shall suggest, have important consequences for armament and disarmament. But in general, and surely in the past, both the United States and the U.S.S.R. built and maintained their armaments with an eye on each other, and in the framework of their competing foreign policies. In traditional power terms, the United States and Russia were the giants, and neither could allow the other a decisive predominance of power. In Cold-War terms, armaments were important instruments in Soviet hopes for expansion, as in United States determination to contain. Armaments served not only by actual use, as in Korea; the threat of the use of weapons, indeed their very existence in the hands of the big powers, has exercised important influence on developments in and between nations.

The logic of deterrence.[12] The disposition to bilateral competition in armaments was accentuated by the fact that almost incidentally armaments acquired a new consequence, if not a new purpose. For, as a result of the new weapons, both the United States and the U.S.S.R. acquired the power to deal mortal blows to each other. Armament had to provide, then, for national survival as well as to promote other concerns of foreign policy.

If armament—and therefore disarmament—in the post-war had to consider interests of basic national survival as well as other goals of foreign policy, it had to reflect too the basic change engendered by the new weapons. Fundamental to armaments policy today is the fact that "defense," in a traditional sense, does not exist. Today, no nation, not even the Soviet Union or the United States, can protect itself against all-out nuclear attack. Against such attack, the "defense" consists almost entirely in the threat of retaliation. The United States relies for its safety on the Soviet awareness that if it attacked, even if it largely destroyed the United States, we will have the force to retaliate and destroy the Soviet Union. The Soviet Union, too, presumably has the weapons to give it, in turn, the security of deterrence.[13]

9

Assuming that the deterrent works, the risk to national survival from intentional all-out attack is eliminated. The significance of the big weapons for the Cold War, for the main struggle between Communist expansionism and Western containment, is less clear. In military terms, there are those who believe that the big weapons on each side have in effect canceled each other. Neither side will wish to risk retaliation by using them. If so, perhaps the Soviet Union can safely push at its rim with conventional weapons, in the hope of quick and easy victories. Korea might have taught, more quickly and more persuasively than it did, that the Communists might start conventional war in the expectation that the West will not resort to nuclear weapons. In fact, if belatedly, the West has recently taken some steps toward strengthening its conventional power to deter or meet such further Soviet thrusts. If it has not done more, part of the reason may be some inclination to a competing view—that Korea was a sport; now, at least, non-nuclear war by the Big Powers is also outdated; so-called conventional war could probably not avoid "tactical nuclear" weapons, and the possibility of limiting wars, if they start, to such weapons is an illusion. Any nation which starts any war is courting all-out war; if so, the deterrent should work to discourage all military adventures.

Whether either argument is "correct," and in what degree, is debated; but, in fact, both sides have continued to build armaments large and small. Perhaps neither has had clearly in mind the actual use for any of them; perhaps both sides have built only for defense and deterrence. But there appeared also political uses for weapons. Soviet armaments have helped keep its satellite empire, and may protect Cuba. In a very different sense, the presence of United States troops has helped keep some countries from possible communist seizure. Weapons too give prestige, an asset in Cold-War competition. Weapons can also be themselves an instrument of competition, when various nations seek to purchase them for their own feuds or defenses. And in other ways, having weapons has seemed to exercise a sure though incalculable influence on the conduct of the Big Powers themselves, and of others. (Of this we shall speak again when we consider why nations have not disarmed.) While neither the Soviet Union nor the United States might have built their weapons for these political purposes alone, political "uses" have not been over-looked in the planning and justification of military programs. Surely, both sides have had much in mind the relevance of their weapons—those used, and those in the background—in civil wars, insurrections, subversions, whether in Cuba, in Laos, in Vietnam.

Of course, if armaments serve the purposes of a nation's foreign policy, changes in that policy will also change the need, the character, the purposes of its armaments. No changes to date, or in prospect, promise any change in the need for those armaments that constitute the major deterrent. But possible changes in the political confrontation which is the Cold War—whether they involve some relaxation of tension, changes within alliances, or just waiting while alliances "shake down"—may lead to changes in armaments arsenals, arms deployment, armaments budgets, armaments planning.

E. *Disarmament in East-West Policies*

Such has been the role of armaments in the pursuit of national survival and other national goals since the last War. The exposition is, of course, too simplified. And we do not stop at all to identify the less-rational, less-planned elements contributing to an arms program or an arms race—the organic character and momentum that they acquire, considerations of domestic politics, domestic economics, personalities, public reaction, and some yet more subtle in influence. In any event, that nations arming heavily in support of adverse interests have nevertheless continued to negotiate to achieve agreement on disarmament is itself remarkable and in need of explanation. It says much for the influence of the United Nations, for the concern of the Big Powers for the opinions of nations, which itself became a focus in the Cold War: other nations have feared a holocaust from Big Power hostilities and have pressed them to seek agreement. The Big Powers saw fit to respond to these pressures. Perhaps, too, they sought some political advantage from the negotiations, or some military advantage from some agreement. In fact, however, many believed that both sides seriously probed the possibilities of agreed disarmament: the Big Powers had a common interest in avoiding nuclear war; they had a common interest, therefore, in avoiding any hostilities; they sought, then, to eliminate or reduce weapons, reduce the risk of unwanted war, and save, too, the crushing burdens of armament.

That despite conflicting foreign policies, disarmament may be in the common interest is not incredible: first, it might remove

11

the ever-present danger of nuclear destruction which faces both the United States and the U.S.S.R. Security through deterrence, through balance of terror, is expensive and terrible. To date, it has "worked," but there are dangers. The other side might upset the stability of the deterrent; it might perhaps achieve a way of destroying its adversary's retaliatory weapons, or develop some defense against them, so as to render itself secure against the threat of retaliation.

There are also dangers inherent in the psychological character of deterrence. Deterrence works only if it works. It does not preclude that a madman might decide to bring the whole structure down; or that some country someday—China?—may conclude that it can survive retaliation and flourish; or that an attacker might be satisfied that the victim will be unable or unwilling to retaliate. There is also ever-present the risk that some accident, or mistake, or miscalculation, might cause one side to launch a nuclear attack; or that some smaller, more conventional war, between big powers or others, will escalate or expand into a big war.

No one can assess the magnitudes of these dangers, or the probabilities that what might happen will happen. What is clear is that if they do occur there will be catastrophe: the most optimistic suggest hundreds of millions dead, many millions maimed and their heredity jeopardized, and the civilization we have known destroyed or set back for many years. Surely such dangers, all would agree, are worth some effort to avoid. Both sides should be eager to end the balance of terror, and free themselves from the constant danger of sudden destruction.

Survival apart, it can be argued that the respective interests in the Cold War might also benefit from disarmament. The big weapons have off-set each other; they have not been used and cannot be used without unacceptable risks and consequences. Their very existence renders dangerous the determined pursuit of competing national interests by nonviolent means. Weapons are expensive to achieve and maintain; they become quickly obsolescent and have to be replaced at tremendous costs. The nations for whose favor East and West are competing desire big power disarmament. The Cold War demands huge sums in foreign aid, which could be provided if defense budgets could be cut. The United States would like to cut taxes; the Soviet Union would like to provide its people with consumer goods. If the other side also gave them up, neither side would need its weapons,

12

whether for national survival or for pursuit of the ideological competition by political or economic means.[14]

The arguments for agreed disarmament seem too obvious and reasonable to need elaboration. Only seventeen years of failure, and uncertain prospects ahead, stand in silent rebuttal. The reasons for failure are not easy to identify or articulate. They lie buried in the traditional policies and habits of nations, in complexities of relations between nations in the years since the Second World War, in Soviet aspirations and the Cold War, in the new technology and the new strategy, in the changing facts and faces of international life.

F. *Seventeen Years of Failure*

We will not detail here the history of the negotiations. It has been told elsewhere fully and well.[15] We glance at that history briefly for the light it might shed on the motivations and interests of East and West, and on the prospects ahead. For some, its discouraging lesson may be that no disarmament is possible between nations in sharp political conflict. This has been summed up in the suggestion that, at all times, at least one side believed that its foreign policy required armaments or excluded disarmament on any basis likely to be acceptable to the other. If so, it has been said, there never has been any real negotiation: despite all the proposals and counter-proposals, the U.N. resolutions, the different forums for negotiation and the changing participants, at least one side was making proposals which the other side could not or was not likely to accept.[16] Disarmament negotiations were not being used, then, by both sides to attempt to find an area of common interest, or some exchange offering each side some compensating advantage. (Of course, the negotiations themselves, though not leading to agreement, may have had important influence on armament and disarmament policies.)

Whether or not one accepts the view that there have been no "real negotiations," the headnotes of the story are illuminating. From 1945 through 1949 the United States had a monopoly of atomic weapons. It offered to give the atom to an international agency for control and peaceful development.[17] The proposal was, one may presume, idealistic and bona fide; if the Soviet Union had agreed, if the U.S. Senate had then given its consent, the story of civilization since might have been markedly different. But perhaps Stalin's Soviet Union could not agree. At that stage, international control would inevitably have entailed a dominant role

13

for the United States. Russia might thereby have been denied even the knowledge of making the bomb, which the United States had; probably, the Soviet Union would have frozen itself into permanent nuclear inferiority. International control pointed also to supra-nationalism and the end of Soviet control of its own destiny and its own security. During American monopoly, then, there was no likelihood of agreement. The Soviet Union's "proposals" consisted of appeals to "Ban the Bomb" and proportional cuts in conventional forces to preserve their superiority for conventional war.

1950-53 was the period of the Korean War, and disarmament negotiations were largely suspended. Opportunities revived with the Korean Armistice, which coincided, roughly, with the death of Stalin and the detonation by the Soviet Union of a hydrogen bomb. Now, perhaps, meaningful negotiations seemed possible. But, as we shall see, for technological reasons, disarmament as once conceived was not possible: the knowledge of how to make the bomb could not be eliminated, and stockpiles could not be discovered. And, in a sense, the race was just beginning. The United States was far ahead. The Soviet Union would not give up and remain far behind. The United States would not sacrifice its advantage. From 1953 to 1957, then, there was perhaps serious negotiation, but only peripheral controls were negotiable. Plans for comprehensive disarmament were indeed offered by both sides, but, in retrospect at least, they had little chance for success. Hopes flared frequently for some partial disarmament, but these too failed. Sometimes it was obvious that a proposal was not in fact in the interest of both sides; sometimes Soviet refusal to accept inspection seemed the obstacle, though that too may have been pretext. Sometimes a proposal acceptable one year was no longer so the next, if it conflicted with new armaments policies; proposals which would be acceptable if some political settlement occurred—say, in regard to Germany—were not acceptable in the absence of settlement. (Decisions to incorporate a rearmed Germany into NATO precluded agreements on "disengagement," and modified troop ceilings which might have been acceptable earlier.)[18] The measures which really interested the United States during this period, were "open skies" and "early warning"— measures against surprise attack. But this did not really interest the Russians. They were apparently confident that we would not attack first; perhaps, too, they had confidence in their military

14

intelligence to apprise them of our intentions. In turn, they were not eager to be inspected, to give up their military advantage of secrecy and perhaps something of their political need for privacy.

In 1958 came Sputnik, bringing new Soviet prestige and new Soviet confidence. Evidence before the world that the Soviet Union apparently had superiority in one technical respect relevant to weaponry did not make the Russians eager to make concessions. For the United States, too, Sputnik only accelerated our incentives to arm rather than our efforts to persuade the Soviet Union to disarm. Both sides continued to make disarmament proposals, but their minds were on an arms race, the Soviet Union trying to match or offset U.S. advantages, the United States concerned particularly over a possible "missile gap."

Finally came Khrushchev's proposal for "General and Complete Disarmament,"[19] and in due course our version of the same.[20] As to the Soviet plan, the United States insisted that it was largely propaganda, not bona fide; that "one cannot get there from here" —one cannot reduce national armaments to levels sufficient only for internal defense in the time suggested by the Russians; that any progressive disarmament had to be in stages, that every stage must leave the United States secure, and at every stage it must be clear that in fact the Soviet Union was carrying out its undertakings; that one could not disarm national forces "generally and completely" unless they could be replaced by an effective and reliable international force to maintain international peace and security. But the U.S. proposals too were proposals which, it could be expected, the Soviet Union would not accept. The early stages suggested by the United States would perpetuate or accentuate the areas of U.S. advantage, or reduce the respects in which the Soviet Union had advantage. They involved, for example, percentile cuts in delivery vehicles which would maintain the substantial lead for the United States; they included measures requiring substantial inspection in the Soviet Union.[21]

The test ban. In recent years the principal efforts and the greatest hopes centered on negotiations to achieve a ban on the testing of nuclear weapons. The earnestness of these negotiations owe as much to chance and improvisation in international politics, as to careful military or political consideration. The Soviet Union, originally, pressed efforts to achieve a test-ban, and an accompanying moratorium on testing, with various possible aims: to promote the Soviet image as the apostle of peace; to keep the United States

15

from spreading nuclear weapons to France and Germany; to slow the development of new weapons by the United States. Eventually, the United States, too, saw corresponding advantages in a test-ban agreement (including the postponement of Communist China's entry into the "Nuclear Weapons Club"), provided Soviet compliance could be effectively monitored. What began, at least in the public mind, as pressure to end the hazards of fall-out and radiation acquired new rationales which were even more promising since they suggested that a ban would promote identical, or parallel, foreign policy interests of both sides.

At various times, it appeared as though agreement was near, but it has not happened. The obstacle to agreement appeared to be "inspection," but one cannot say with confidence whether this has been the real issue. In the United States it seemed that at least some of the voices insisting on high levels of "inspection" believed also that the test ban itself might not be in the interest of the United States.[22] The Soviet Union which once seemed eager for agreement, then seemed reluctant. It was not clear whether the Kremlin had decided that a ban was not in the Russian interest, or whether Soviet leaders felt that the ban was not worth the inspection which the United States required. Or, perhaps, the Russians really believed that the test ban could be adequately monitored without inspection, and saw United States insistence on inspection as having other motivations. Soviet refusal to agree to a ban on tests in the atmosphere alone,[23] which could be monitored from afar and would require no internal inspection, only confused estimates as to their intention. But the test ban negotiations remained alive, and recently the Soviet Union flared hopes for agreement by reopening negotiations about the amounts of inspection, although at this writing the parties are not within reach of agreement.[24]

G. *Why Nations Have Not Disarmed*

Seventeen years of failure suggest that the arguments "proving" that disarmament is in the interest of both the Soviet Union and the United States must not tell the whole story. At least one side, some would say both, found more persuasive the reasons for keeping weapons and even increasing them at tremendous cost, or at least for not entering into a disarmament agreement. Partial reasons are implicit in the story of the negotiations; other reasons can only be guessed at, but they seem worth speculation.

16

A "sophisticated" explanation for the lack of any comprehensive agreement on disarmament is that nations do not throw on the bargaining table, and put out of their own control, the "basics" of national survival. The skepticism about disarmament which has come to many with years of frustration existed from the beginning with some traditional diplomatists and masters of "real politik," who found no serious disarmament in their own experience or in diplomatic history and had no room for it in their theories of how nations behave. Perhaps, for a while, the terrible War and the awesome new atomic bomb, which moved nations to create the United Nations, might possibly have moved them to the even more radical adjustments of comprehensive disarmament under supra-national controls, like that called for by the original Acheson-Lilienthal Plan of 1946 for international control of the atom.[25] But that it did not happen then suggests that nothing has happened to make nations change their ways. To date, these skeptics can, of course, say they told us so.

Those who do not accept that nations are inherently beyond this "salvation," may yet recognize that only unusual fears and crises move nations to radical readjustments, and comprehensive, supervised disarmament with its political consequences would be radical indeed. One might have thought, perhaps, that the big weapons would shake the inertia of nations, but it has not happened. Perhaps one adequate explanation is that both sides have come to believe that big weapons cannot in fact be disarmed. How to make a bomb is knowledge that cannot be eradicated, and some groups, somewhere, some day, can start to make one. Nuclear stockpiles, also, can be hidden beyond the reach of any practicable detection, and even delivery vehicles can be "hardened" and made difficult to destroy or detect. Against these dangers, no nation will wish to give up its nuclear deterrent, unless perhaps it were replaced by some yet-to-be devised, effective, and reliable international force beyond the ken of present political planning.[26] And so, the ultimate deterrent, at least, is not up for negotiation. Then, if big weapons are here to stay, they are accepted. Governments and peoples, the Big Powers themselves as well as others, have seemed to experience only infrequent twinges of desperation. They have seemed hardly, and rarely, concerned about the risks inherent in mutual deterrence. Despite the obvious—that one side or the other can, in minutes, devastate the planet—both sides have appeared sanguine that it will not happen. That we have been living with the big weapons has bred confidence that we can continue to live with them. And, with the big fear largely inoperative, traditional attitudes in diplomacy and strategy have tended to prevail. Then, other "uses" for armaments began to weigh more heavily. Military establishments have tended to have confidence in what they have, and the possession of a mighty arsenal has bred a sense of security, even if not quite justified. Political leaders, too, have found that the mere possession of big weapons gave confidence to their postures and stirred hesitation in their opponents.[27] It appears likely, for example, that the Soviet Union acted "tougher" about Berlin, and we were more cautious and sober, when both sides thought there was a "missile gap" in Russia's favor; the postures almost reversed when our continued superiority became clear. (Some people apparently believe that our recent success in Cuba was due in large part to the fact that although neither side desired or expected nuclear war, we were in a position to "rattle" our big weapons more loudly. While this assessment is not beyond question, the fact that people believe that our success was due to our nuclear "superiority" will cause them to be reluctant to reduce this superiority in first steps of disarmament, even to trade it for other advantages.)[28]

Of course, assuming that some big weapons as an ultimate deterrent are today beyond the reach of disarmament, there are yet strong arguments for first steps and partial measures. But without the big fear, we have said, a major impetus to agreement is lacking. In a context of cold war, traditional attitudes push instead to traditional measures—to cementing alliances and building up weapons. Both sides, moreover, have apparently felt generally secure in their present position in world affairs, and able to plan in a context which is familiar; neither has been confident that it could imagine accurately what the world would look like if disarmament in some degree were put into effect. In the context of continuing conflict between them, it has not been clear to either how disarmament would affect its capabilities for economic and political competition between them. At best, then, the advantages of disarmament have been uncertain; for the United States they might have involved also the sacrifice of some present superiorities; from the Soviet Union they would have required also the price of inspection. Only if both sides wished to relax or modify the Cold War, might the advantages of disarmament clearly outweigh its uncertainties. And if they were ready to relax the Cold War, it may be argued, some reciprocal disarmament would indeed begin to happen, even without complicated agreements.

Inspection. We have mentioned "inspection" as an obstacle to agreed disarmament; in fact inspection has often appeared as the main issue, explaining the failure to achieve agreement. But, as suggested in relation to the Test Ban negotiations, it has never been wholly clear whether and when inspection was the text or the pretext: when, as in the corresponding case of Americans who demand needlessly high levels of inspection, Soviet failure to agree to adequate inspection might have been its method of refusing to agree to substance; when substantive agreement might have been acceptable to the Soviet Union but it was not worth the price of inspection.

It might seem unlikely that inspection could be a real issue, but inevitably the United States had to assume it was. In any event, inspection became constantly entangled with the substantive limitations under negotiation. Limitations that could not be verified could not be negotiated. And uncertainty as to the reasons for Soviet resistance to inspection inevitably colored the negotiations. To some, Soviet resistance to inspection was clear evidence of an intent to remain free to violate. To others, it was, rather— consistent with an intent to observe the agreement—a fear that its closed society could not stand scrutiny by foreigners; or that, at least, its interest in the substantive controls was not sufficiently great to be worth the price of inspection. The Soviet Union also considered its closed society and its effective secrecy a military advantage; it was not willing to give it up except for a corresponding military advantage.

Finally, we repeat, there are those "reasons" why disarmament has not occurred which correspond to some of the less-logical factors which contributed to the arms race. If politics, personalities, public opinion, habit, and general momentum help explain the arms program, they are factors which cannot be omitted in any explanation of the failures of disarmament efforts. To identify and evaluate them is another, too difficult, matter which cannot even be attempted here.

H. *The Prospects*

The array of possible reasons for reluctance to disarm are mere guesses at what may have motivated the powers. Likely, neither

19

side has determined or even probed the consequences of disarmament, since governments are probably no more rational than men in acting according to the balance of the relevant considerations. Those who would speculate as to the future, too, can only attempt to line up and assess the factors for and against. In sum, they may not appear encouraging. But hopes for disarmament, may yet find plausible support in new factors, or in old factors acquiring new importance.

Again, what we are guessing at is whether both sides may yet conclude that their national interests, as they see them, will be promoted as well or better by agreed disarmament. We ask whether the common interest in survival might yet suggest to both sides that some agreement is better than none. We attempt to assay whether there may be changes in foreign policy which may suggest some agreed disarmament instead of arms race.

1. *Today's Weapons and Their Uses.* While international relations and foreign policies seem fluid again, the needs of survival reflected in weapons programs promise no early dramatic change. The felt need for defense by deterrence, we may expect, will continue, and will remain an obstacle to total disarmament. It would not, however, preclude lesser, even comprehensive agreements.

To attempt to anticipate whether the United States and the Soviet Union might yet agree to substitute disarmament, or controlled armaments, for a largely uncontrolled arms race, it is important to know and understand the weapons themselves and their uses, and where the race has left both sides at this time. For most of us this would be a forbiddingly complex inquiry into military strategy and its political uses; we are debarred from it also by the fact that we know neither the character and capabilities of some of the weapons on either side, nor their quantities or deployments. Still, one can garner from the newspapers and periodicals enough about the weaponry of East and West[29] to help understanding of the disarmament problem, of why one side or the other might make a particular proposal, whether the other side could even consider it, what would be some of the more obvious consequences of a particular agreement.

In general, it seems to be the case that the United States has a stockpile of nuclear weapons of varying sizes several times that of the Soviet Union; the Soviet Union may have several very large weapons. The United States, too, has substantially more intercontinental ballistic missiles and long-range heavy bombers. (While the Soviet Union has developed greater "thrust," as reflected in its feats in space, this superiority has no certain military advantage today.) The Soviet Union, on the other hand, has more of the less expensive intermediate-range ballistic missiles and aircraft. The United States, then, could hit the U.S.S.R. very hard and achieve terrible destruction despite the size of the Soviet Union, either by ICBM's from bases in the United States, or by shorter range missiles from European bases or from submarines. (The shorter range weapons presumably have greater accuracy.) Giving up the European bases would probably not appreciably reduce the power of the United States to devastate the Soviet Union, although it may affect other kinds of military activity and might have important political consequences. The Soviet Union with comparatively few ICBM's can probably still inflict devastation in the United States by being more selective about its targets. (Cuban bases would also have brought areas of the United States within reach of Soviet IRBM's; in the future Soviet submarines might achieve this instead.) In particular, the Soviet Union, with its plenty of shorter range missiles, can hit Europe, and to that extent Europe has been hostage for the West.

For so-called conventional warfare, the U.S.S.R. has a large and well-equipped land army augmented by satellite armies and considerable reserves; it also enjoys geographical advantages on the land mass of Europe-Asia and the benefits of centralized control. The West is politically less unified, has smaller forces in being and its reserves include those of the United States, which would have to be transported across the seas. The West, however, has superiority in "battlefield nuclear weapons" including rockets with a range of 200-300 miles. The West also has naval superiority. And it may have the political advantages which have direct military consequences, e.g., the questionable reliability of satellite armies and of satellite populations.

This comparison of military power might suggest, then, that the Soviet bloc (even without Communist China) has an advantage in traditional conventional terms, which is offset by Western superiority in modern weapons, both in tactical weapons and ultimate weapons in the background. This would explain the success of Western "containment" in military terms. It may explain, indeed, why the West continues to dominate politically areas (e.g., Iran, Turkey) which the Soviet Union could dominate

21

by conventional military means: the U.S.S.R., presumably, is deterred by Western nuclear power; in some areas effective Western naval superiority is additional deterrent.

This is the character of the military confrontation, and many commentators would probably consider it generally stable enough at present. The big weapons deter each other; Soviet nuclear domination of Europe is offset by United States nuclear superiority, both intercontinental and over-all. United States nuclear superiority offsets also Soviet conventional superiority, and fear that they may escalate to nuclear war has been an important deterrent to conventional adventures. Most experts do not foresee early important new developments in "anti-missile-missiles," which might again make possible real "defense," and upset the basic stability. Outer space too promises as yet no economical and reliable uses which might disturb the balance. Biological and chemical weapons are not seriously feared as long as there is a nuclear deterrent.

If one considers the uses of force, not for all-out war, nuclear or conventional, but for subversion, fomenting insurrections, initiating, maintaining or intervening in civil wars, both sides have men and weapons aplenty. Skills, experience and allegiance, particularly of local forces and populations, are another matter; these may not be principally a question of armaments, and might not be appreciably affected by the existing array of armaments, or by probable kinds of disarmament.[30]

If military specialists have difficulty estimating the outcome of a particular war, at a particular time and place between particular nations, political specialists have even more difficulty assessing the effect of having particular weapons on the foreign policies of various nations. They sense, but cannot calculate, either, what would be the political consequences of disarmament in varying degrees.

2. *The Modest Promises of Disarmament.* Above are the uses of armaments in the foreign policies of East and West, and so long as the foreign policies remain largely unchanged, the question is whether these uses can be served as well by disarmament. (We assume, perhaps too lightly, that the non-rational reasons for armament and against disarmament can be overcome.) Foremost, a disarmament agreement to be acceptable would have to enhance basic stability; surely it must not disturb it. For the foreseeable future, clearly, neither side will agree to sacrifice its ultimate deterrent weapons. At present, too, the Soviet Union

22

will be reluctant to sacrifice its conventional superiority; the United States will be reluctant to sacrifice its nuclear superiority. The question is whether the United States, instead of pursuing some uncertain hope to a "breakthrough" to ultimate superiority,[31] might exchange some reduction in its nuclear superiority (which some consider already "unnecessary" and a rapidly wasting asset) for reductions in Soviet conventional power. Both sides might also agree to reductions—perhaps very substantial reductions—in "numbers," where the reductions would not disturb the balance, say in some kinds of nuclear weapons or delivery vehicles. Such reductions would not alter the basic character of the military confrontation. It would not hamper the pursuit of the present foreign policies of East and West. There may yet be also agreements to slow the spread of nuclear weapons. It is not out of the question that there may be agreements limiting the military uses of outer space.

And there may yet be a test ban. To most observers the test ban has had interest, and promise, as a way of controlling the "Nth country problem"—the spread of weapons to others in either camp, or elsewhere. If the Big Powers give up testing, it has been thought, others will too; and since scientific and military experts in these countries will not develop or rely on weapons they cannot test, prohibitions on testing will in effect inhibit the development of nuclear weapons. The assumption that, if the United States and the U.S.S.R. agree, others will have to join, may never have been warranted and may now be even less confident; one may doubt, in particular, whether France and Communist China would adhere. (Many other nations would indeed accept, some perhaps even happy to be denied the responsibility of facing the difficult decision, whether to join the nuclear "club.")

Whether or not a test ban would control the development of weapons by other countries, some see in it a way of slowing down research and development of new weapons by the Big Powers. And while in itself this involves no disarmament—no elimination or reduction in weapons—it would be a "first step," a token of agreement and a proving ground for further disarmament negotiation, for drafting a disarmament treaty, for establishing inspection or other verification through national or international institutions.

Whether both sides will be willing to take even these small first steps is yet to be seen. There are some reasons to hope for them. There are, always, the dangers inherent in deterrence which can be reduced by relaxation of political tension. At the periphery of the consciousness of military planners occasionally there must lurk, too, the vague uneasiness that the future holds yet more terrible weapons beyond their imagination and control, and that now is the last chance to prevent them. The growing costs of weapons, the constant obsolescence and need to replace, the competing demands in national budgets, the eagerness of the United States to reduce taxes, of the Soviet Union to brighten the drabness of its people's lives by consumer goods, may yet exert a telling if secondary influence to seek some agreement. And the uneasiness of the Big Powers over the spread of weapons to other nations may yet lead them to take initiatives involving formal agreements entailing some controls on the Big Powers as well.

Perhaps, too, as the test ban negotiations indicate, inspection is becoming less of an obstacle to agreement than it has appeared. No one can speak with assurance on how much inspection has weighed in Soviet policy. But, for perhaps the first time, voices are urging that it is time to find out.[32] Surely, they say, it would be desirable to see whether, if the "price" of inspection to the Soviet Union (and ultimately, too, to the United States) could be reduced, Russia might be pushed to agreement on substantive disarmament provisions that are also in the interest of the United States. As is described more fully below, with technological advance, many limitations can be monitored from outside the host territory; others can be monitored with only minimal access to the territory. If the United States should begin to emphasize for negotiation those controls or reductions which could be monitored without major inspection, the prospects of progress might improve. (At least we would have a clearer idea to what extent "inspection" is in fact an obstacle to agreement.)

3. *Political Change and Disarmament Prospects.* These modest steps—a test ban, reductions in existing weapons, agreements to slow the arms race, to curtail the spread of nuclear weapons, to "disarm" outer space—are all that even optimists expect within the context of the foreign policies we have known. Even agreement within a Cold War would presumably have special political motivations. The United States is committed to the principle of disarmament; even domestically, disarmament agreement would have some political impetus, and opposition. For Russia, perhaps some agreement would respond to Soviet interests in its difficulties

24

with China; perhaps to needs within the Soviet Union. But if in fact some agreement comes, one may expect the Cold War, will inevitably be affected, whether or not the parties desire it. The arms race is itself a source and a focus of the Cold War, as well as its consequence. Any indication that the race may slow down will have incalculable effects on alliances, on East-West relations, on areas of tension around the world, on prospects for further agreement.

In fact, many believe it unrealistic to expect even small agreements—even a test ban, surely further "first steps"—unless both sides are seeking some détente. Such agreement will signal a desire or a willingness by both the Soviet Union and the United States to turn the head of the arms race. If so, it may portend further relaxations in other fields of conflict; and although the armaments race may be affected in important ways, formal agreements on disarmament may not be the most important manifestation of this détente. But a desire to moderate the Cold War would surely enhance the prospects of some agreement on disarmament. Disarmament is already the subject of negotiation; it need not involve sacrifice of important interests; it carries immediate kudos and perhaps some political advantage; it promises—less quickly than some hope—important economic benefits.

Views may differ as to whether the Soviet Union in fact desires a relaxation of the Cold War, or whether there are in process other political developments, in or out of Russia, which may improve the prospects of some disarmament agreement. What does appear, at this writing, is that important political changes are in progress, though their relevance to armaments and disarmament cannot yet be discerned or appreciated. The bi-polar character of post-war international relations, we have said, is much modified. New nations go an independent way without effective fear of the Big Powers and their big weapons. Alliances on both sides are being shaken, although the Cold War has not yet been radically affected. France, a key ally of the United States and a linchpin of NATO, is increasingly going a separate way and is pursuing hopes of an independent nuclear deterrent; it will take a disarmament agreement different from those we have suggested to persuade France to give up her quest for significant independence. And disturbances in the Western alliance are not likely, in any event, to improve prospects for disarmament. If the Soviet Union had been contemplating some détente it might now decide to wait to see what she might gain instead from the troubled waters of the Western alliance. That she might even offer some disarmament, in a form which would further divide the allies, is conceivable, but less probable.

On the other hand, for the Soviet Union, there is China. Sino-Soviet differences, if they persist, promise important consequences for Soviet foreign policy, perhaps even for its relations with the West. That these would include early East-West agreement on major disarmament is highly unlikely; indeed, if relations with China worsen seriously, both the United States and the U.S.S.R. might begin to look in that direction and to think of policies quite other than disarmament. On the other hand, some small agreements between the United States and the U.S.S.R. may serve the interests of the United States as well as some political purposes of the Soviet Union in its difficulties with China; a test ban, for example, we have suggested, might help show to the Communist world the successes of co-existence, and justify Soviet refusals to aid Chinese nuclear armament. And Chinese-Soviet differences may also affect an old obstacle to agreement. It has always been assumed that important disarmament would require the participation of China. It was also assumed that if the U.S.S.R. wished a particular agreement, it could produce China's adherence as well. Now differences between the U.S.S.R. and China are sufficiently acute to cast doubt on whether China would join any disarmament agreement. But, on the other hand, Chinese—and French—non-participation may no longer be as serious an obstacle to U.S.-Soviet agreement. In sum, continued Soviet-Chinese difficulties may tend to improve prospects for some disarmament agreement, while continued uncertainties in the Western camp may tend to encourage Russia, instead, to wait and watch.

I. *Disarmament and the Other Nations*

We return to an earlier *caveat*. We have discussed disarmament in the foreign policies of East and West. These two, with their "super-power," have bestrode the world since 1945. These two have constituted the context of disarmament negotiations from the beginning. All discussions of the subject concentrate on East-West disarmament. Other nations in the United Nations voting, easily if earnestly, for resolutions calling for disarmament have in mind East-West disarmament, particularly in regard to super-weapons. They might have other thoughts if disarmament

26

should reach down into the weapons which they—Indonesia, India, Pakistan, Egypt, Israel—have been building up for their own purposes.

The bi-lateral aspect may still be the important focus for discussions of disarmament. The United States and Russia alone are effectively negotiating about disarmament. Any small steps which the Big Two may decide to take are theirs to take, and might be taken regardless of others, even of France and of Communist China. But if disarmament is to go on, if bigger reductions are to be contemplated, even the Big Powers, *inter se*, may soon have to realize that there are factors in the disarmament picture other than their own competing aspirations. In fact, they may conclude that, even if verification were not an insuperable obstacle to elimination of the big weapons, it is these weapons which make them superior powers; these should be kept, not merely to deter each other but to influence others. If the Big Two do begin to negotiate about substantial reductions in any weapons, they may be compelled to insist that other countries—in addition to France and China—also begin to lay their armaments on the table, whether or not these include nuclear weapons. This would add to the disarmament tangle the foreign policies of other nations and the reasons why they have acquired their arms. If the United States and the U.S.S.R. were agreed about other issues, say about the Middle East or Kashmir, they might indeed be able to compel the countries involved to make a start towards disarmament. So long as they are not, the relevance of other powers at some not-too-late stage of negotiation may only further aggravate the difficulties of comprehensive disarmament.

II. THE SPECIAL CONCERNS OF THE LAWYER

The lawyer, we have suggested, is concerned with disarmament in common with his fellow citizens. He has, too, special professional interests that concern him in particular. Of course, the international lawyer is professionally concerned with disarmament insofar as it relates to international law and international order. He is concerned with the drafting, interpretation, and implementation of international disarmament agreements, and with the settlement of disputes arising out of these agreements. He is concerned with the creation and operation of institutions, national or international, for the administration of disarmament programs, for dealing with alleged violations of disarmament agreements. He is concerned, too, with the operation of law and institutions to settle political controversy and maintain international peace and security in a disarmed or a disarming world. The American lawyer must consider too the impact of disarmament agreements applied in the United States on our laws and institutions, on the operations of government, on the rights of persons and corporations. He will be concerned, finally, with laws and programs designed to alleviate the economic dislocation that might follow, for a while, upon certain disarmament agreements.

A. Armaments and International Law

There is no accepted principle of international law against the proliferation of armaments. At one time, it might have been possible to interpret the Charter of the United Nations as forbidding the possession of major armaments (except perhaps if clearly for defensive purposes), as a violation of the undertaking to refrain from the "threat of force." But the retention of armaments, by the Big Powers at least, was part of the scheme of the Charter. They were to have arms, and make some available to the United Nations for purposes of enforcing the peace. Originally, disarmament and the regulation of armaments were only possible later developments about which the General Assembly might make recommendations (Article 11). Surely, the mere retention of arms by the Big Powers was not forbidden. Even for others, as the law has developed, at least some additional active threat, expressed or implied, to use weapons aggressively seems necessary to constitute a "threat of force."

B. Disarmament Agreements and Their Enforcement

Disarmament, then, comes into law only as nations agree to it, and disarmament agreements would be the concern of the lawyer in the same ways as other international agreements. He must help draft the treaties, include provisions for bringing them into effect, provide for the settlement of disputes about their interpretation or application. But, in addition, the negotiation of disarmament agreements since the Second World War has given large importance to problems which previously had not seemed serious: how to induce

28

nations to observe an agreement, how to verify whether nations have complied, how to plan particularly for charges and denials of violation, how to prepare for the possibility that an agreement might be violated.

These problems are not novel; it is their importance which is new, as is the concern of nations to wrestle with them. In international agreements generally, even in the few disarmament agreements of the past, it was assumed that nations would comply; that if they did not, the violation would be obvious or soon discovered; that the victim of the breach would avail himself of the usual remedies—rescission of the agreement, claims for damages, perhaps both. If the treaty was important enough the victim might react in ways not directly related, by reprisals or even by going to war. Apart from his "remedy" for the breach, the victim might also take measures to overcome any advantage gained by the violator. In the negotiation of disarmament agreements today, nations are for virtually the first time in peace (as distinguished from agreements with vanquished nations) dropping the traditional politesse of international behaviour: they are seeking inspection in the territory of other sovereign nations; they frankly assert that other parties to the agreement cannot be trusted to comply; they anticipate the measures to be taken in response to a breach.

New international attitudes towards possible violations have required nations to begin new studies of the behaviour of nations. Lawyers have been among the first students of the problems of enforcement of disarmament agreements among sovereign nations. They have applied familiar lessons from the jurisprudence of domestic law; they have recognized important differences.

1. *Inducing Nations to Observe Disarmament Agreements.* The common assumption that inspection is necessary—and adequate—to assure that the Soviet Union will abide by its agreements is too simple.[33] The overwhelming majority of international agreements are observed by all nations, without any inspection or "enforcement machinery" whatever. Disarmament agreements are not necessarily different. For any nation which concludes a disarmament agreement there are important reasons for observing it. A disarmament agreement will come only if the parties are satisfied that it is in their interest. If the advantages, international or domestic, are worth obtaining they are worth keeping; they will not be quickly or lightly jeopardized by a violation which would cause the other side to abrogate the agreement. States, like the U.S.S.R. and the

U.S., which compete for world influence, will not lightly break a disarmament agreement in which other nations have keen interest. In addition, agreements which come into effect acquire a life and a momentum, introducing changes in practices and in attitudes of nations which cannot lightly be reversed. It is not always easy for a nation to terminate an agreement even when the right to renounce has been expressly reserved. (Recall the difficulties which the United States encountered in terminating the test-ban moratorium.) There are also institutional and societal forces within every nation, including the Soviet Union, impelling it to live up to agreements which it has signed.

The forces motivating nations—even the Soviet Union— to observe agreements—even agreements affecting national security—are not to be discounted. Lawyers have also suggested that inducements to comply can be strengthened,[34] some even artificially created, *e.g.*, by compliance bonds in escrow, or even that ancient practice, the exchange of hostages. One might also increase the motivation to comply by exploiting domestic institutions; for example, by requiring appropriate periodic declarations by the chiefs of state, or working the obligation to comply into the internal laws and institutions of a country.

Any additional inducements to comply which could be developed would be welcome, and might increase the likelihood of reaching agreement. But additional reliable inducements are not easy to come by. Proposals for inducing compliance must be such as will induce compliance by the Russians—not merely those which would induce us to comply. They must not only be calculated to induce compliance but also give confidence to the United States that they will do so. "Gimmicks" do not breed confidence and are not politically acceptable to either side. And enforcement schemes must be reciprocal; some of the things which the United States might like to see done in the Soviet Union, we could not agree to do in the United States.

2. *If a Violation Occurs.* Regardless of other reasons why the Soviet Union might observe a disarmament agreement, to the United States it appears that fear of detection, and of what the United States would do in response to a violation, would be a major deterrent to Soviet violation. For political as well as for security reasons, the United States requires confidence that important violations will be detected, that such violations will not cause serious, irreparable damage to the United States, that re-

30

sponses will be available to undo the damage to the national interest resulting from any agreement broken by the other side.

3. *Verification and Inspection.* U.S. disarmament policy, we have said, has had at its core the need for inspection to verify Soviet compliance with any disarmament measures which might be negotiated. Every attempt at agreement foundered, or seemed to founder, in large part on U.S. demand for and Soviet rejection of inspection. But increasingly it has been recognized[35] that inspection is not a principle but the means to a desired end; that the end—knowledge whether there has been a violation—can frequently be achieved by means other than what we usually think of as "inspection"; that verification itself is only a means to a further end—inducing the Soviet Union to abide by an agreement—and that verification does not itself assure such Soviet compliance and might not be the principal inducement to compliance. In the Test Ban negotiations, for example, we no longer even ask for inspection of a ban on atmospheric tests, since we can monitor them from afar, unilaterally. In the case of the Korean armistice, on the other hand, we have known of Communist violations of some provisions, but our knowledge of these violations has not deterred the Communists; it has made it possible for the United Nations Command in Korea to respond by also disregarding the provisions violated.

Over the years, the insistence upon inspection has perhaps become encrusted with other motives and purposes. Some see in inspection in the Soviet Union a source of military intelligence; some a way of opening up Soviet society; others have set hopes upon inspection as a vehicle for establishing, developing, and enhancing international institutions. These may all be desirable purposes, but they are extraneous to disarmament policy. To insist on inspection for these purposes when it is not needed, sets up additional obstacles to agreement on disarmament and arms control measures which are in the interest of the United States.

It has been suggested that controls which can be monitored unilaterally, from the outside, since they would involve least penetration into Soviet territory and Soviet society, offer the best hopes for first steps towards some disarmament.[36] (Agreements which can be verified without, or with minimum, access to the territory of the other side will also raise less problems in the implementation, both in the Soviet Union and in the United States.) At least, such proposals would help test whether to the Soviet Union inspection is the serious obstacle, or is only a pretext

31

for refusing substantive controls. That knowledge would be important to the formulation of American disarmament policy, and would also help the United States in its propaganda battles with Russia. Inevitably, however, as disarmament progresses, it will be necessary to provide for inspection of varying kind and thoroughness in the territory of the parties to the agreement. Different possible inspection systems are being studied and debated.

4. *Organization of Inspection Systems.* Verification systems must, of course, be effective. They must inform, with a sufficient degree of confidence, whether there has been a violation. An inspecting system must also be largely immune to sabotage or frustration which could break the system down and make it impossible to know whether there has been a violation.

These are largely technical concerns, but they also have important political components. Lawyers have been concerned with the political and legal organization of these systems. They have helped outline organizational schemes; they have been alert, too, to the need to assure that systems be politically acceptable, both at the negotiating table and in subsequent operation. For many years it was assumed that an inspection system had to be "international" or "impartial." Recently it has been recognized that particularly for agreements operating solely or principally between the United States and the U.S.S.R. (or between NATO and the Warsaw Pact countries) many problems could be avoided by having "reciprocal inspection"—one side inspecting the other.[37] This would eliminate complex organizations, the effort to agree on rules for their membership, operation, governance, budgeting, the need to find trained neutral or impartial personnel. Each side would also, presumably, have more confidence in its own inspectors than in neutrals who, in addition to lacking the same motivations to uncover violations, will, for political reasons, tend to err on the side of finding "non-violation." Impartial or neutral inspection personnel may, on the other hand, be politically more acceptable, particularly in the United States, and their findings would have greater credibility if violation is to bring some organized response from the international community. It may be possible, too, to create mixed systems having some of the advantages of unilateral, reciprocal and international inspection.

For later stages of disarmament involving many countries, an international disarmament agency has been projected.[38] Details have still to be chiseled out, apparently even within the U.S.

government; negotiation and agreement surely are yet far ahead. Some of the problems to be anticipated have already appeared in the test-ban negotiations, *e.g.,* the problems of impartial administration. (The Russians suggested a Troika there, even before they asked for a three-headed Secretary-General for the United Nations.) Proposals made by the United States in recent negotiations contemplate a "constitution" for an International Disarmament Organization, which in addition to administration would have a "Control Council," a political body for which there will have to be agreed functions, powers, voting procedures, and a General Conference, a larger body, for which again there will need to be rules for membership, operation, functions.[39]

Even more than other agreements, disarmament will have to struggle with the problem of settling disputes in the application of the agreement; an inspection system and an inspection organization, in particular, will inevitably breed disputes. To the domestic lawyer, the obvious answer is the judicial or arbitral process, and indeed some kinds of issues might lend themselves to such methods. But the mass of issues arising in the daily operation of inspection systems would not be justiciable, nor could they await the leisurely judicial determination of law or of facts. A conclusion that there has been a substantive violation, or serious sabotage of the inspection system, will be a political determination on more-or-less ambiguous scientific data. Such a conclusion will presumably be reached quickly, principally by the victim of the breach, in the first instance, then by international political bodies if the victim seeks political action from them. The task for the draftsman and the negotiator is to achieve not ideal, optimal systems, but practical ones that will be negotiable, that will work, that will deter violations, that will give confidence to each side that if a violation occurs the victim will know it and be in a position to safeguard its interests.

5. *Responses.* Lawyers have long dealt with sanctions and remedies for violations of private agreements. In international agreements, particularly in disarmament agreements, the adequacy of available remedies may be critical. Writers have come to speak of reactions to such violations as "responses," including not only legal remedies or political sanctions, but whatever the victim does in reaction to a known or suspected violation.[40]

Response to a violation of an international agreement may range of course from total war to doing nothing. One purpose of a response is "restorative," to prevent or repair or mitigate any damage to the national interest from the violation and from the violated agreement. Confidence that there would be an adequate restorative response may be essential if a country is to go into an agreement affecting vital interests. Also, the fact that the victim has the ability to restore his situation will generally help deter a violation. Often an adequate restorative is for the victim in turn to abrogate the agreement, but if the agreement was worthwhile, and if the violation has not utterly destroyed the value of the agreement, the victim may not wish to tear it up and might seek some less drastic remedy.

Responses may also have retaliatory or punitive purposes, and frequently there will be popular demand for "retribution." Unilateral or allied retaliation, reprisal or "punishment," may often be feasible, and in the case of serious violations restorative and retributive motives may blend to support drastic responses. But one cannot count heavily on international punishment, even if the international community accepts that there has been a violation. Nations other than the immediate victim have been reluctant to punish each other,[41] especially since some forms of sanctions— economic sanctions, for instance—may inflict suffering also on the punisher and on others besides the offender.

The punishment of individuals responsible for violations raises different questions. Violators of disarmament agreements, it should be clear, cannot be handled by judicial machinery, national or international, like that invoked or proposed for private "international crimes"—piracy, slavery, white slavery, smuggling, narcotics. The important violation of a disarmament agreement will not be that of the outlaw running weapons for private gain. The violations that matter are violations by governmental authorities of major states. If they should occur, the relevant precedent would be not "piracy" but Nuremberg, and one may again wish to consider Nuremberg-type trials. One may seriously question, however, whether it is desirable to seek agreement for that contingency in disarmament negotiations. It is hardly likely that either the United States or the Soviet Union would now agree to such trials for governmental leaders in the event of a violation of a disarmament agreement.

C. *Maintaining the Peace in a Disarming World*

Disarmament is intended as a means to international peace and stability; it should not of course become instead a source of instability and an invitation to aggression. That was what happened between World Wars when other countries disarmed while Hitler's Germany rearmed. Few can say with confidence that it would not happen again if the West disarmed unilaterally while the Communist bloc retained its offensive power.

Similar considerations, we have said, motivate American insistence that at every stage in the disarmament process, and at its end, the security of the United States should not be jeopardized. The Soviet Union, of course, also has these concerns, and nominally at least both sides have agreed that stages in the process of disarmament should give neither side any military advantage. In the early stages of any foreseeable agreement, both sides will have their deterrent for their ultimate security. They will still have, too, lesser weapons to implement other foreign policy interests as they see them. But if the process of disarmament is to continue there will have to be other changes. Further steps—like the first steps—will take place only if nations conclude that disarmament serves them better than the maintenance of armaments. Inevitably, steps towards arms control or disarmament will reflect—and cause—some relaxation of hostility. And political change may mean opportunity for the lawyer to seize some occasion for strengthening the fabric of international order, increasing the area of agreement on rules of conduct for nations, improving machinery for the settlement of disputes.[42] It may not be possible to build a "rule of law" community as long as the international scene does not represent common interests and values. It may be possible to implement by law those narrow sectors where there are common interests, *e.g.,* avoidance of war, some disarmament, reciprocal trade and cultural exchange.

To many, we have said, moderate disarmament and concomitant moderate relaxation of tensions are all that can be hoped for in the years ahead. In fact, both the United States and the U.S.S.R. have seen fit to offer "blueprints" for general and complete disarmament, down to levels sufficient only for internal police. Of course, if one dismisses these as propagandistic or utopian, one need not plan for those last stages or negotiate about them. But for the United States at least, launching such a proposal even in the most

35

general terms suggests good faith commitment in principle and some intention to consider it in detail. Lawyers must help, both by distinguishing ideal societies from minimal political adjustment, and by lending their skills to each of these different undertakings.[43]

General and complete disarmament down to a level sufficient only for internal police would leave a situation difficult to imagine, perhaps one fraught with instabilities. With weapons eliminated, different powers might become the "big powers," factors other than military power would become more important determinants of international influence. If one accepts such "complete disarmament" as a realistic possibility, one can only speculate as to the prospects for peace; will nations fight with the small weapons they have left? What would happen to Soviet satellites? Will there be more or fewer instances of insurrection and subversion, more or fewer civil wars as in Vietnam and Laos?

Accepting that such a world might come about, some may suggest that even if it would be riddled with instabilities, it is better than what we have: at least there will be no danger of thermonuclear war, no threat to civilization and to the human race. Others insist, however, that such instability is not tolerable. Official United States policy has it that in a disarming world, national forces should give way to effective international police force to maintain international peace and stability.[44] This force must be strong enough to overcome any national power or likely combination of powers. In present "planning" it is assumed that the United Nations would be developed or converted into an effective police organization commanding the necessary power against all outlaws.

Again, lawyers are in the forefront of projecting such a United Nations; lawyers too are in the forefront of debate as to the realism and feasibility of such plans.[45] Will nations ever give up reliance on their own weapons and give them to a supra-national body? How can one establish an international body strong enough to maintain peace, effective when it is needed, but not too strong for the liberties of nations? How can one assure command and control which is reliable and immune to subversion and seizure by hostile forces? Fundamentally, can one build institutions "from the top" without that community of interest which alone can support law or government?

Beyond the development of peace-keeping institutions and machinery, the disarming world will have to strengthen the fabric of international law. New substantive rules will have to be developed, acceptable to the mass of nations, old and new. And new procedures, perhaps new institutions, for settling disputes, so that the world without force will not be one where international wrongs remain unrectified and unrequited.[46]

D. *Disarmament and United States Law*

Virtually neglected have been the problems for the American lawyer arising from the application of a disarmament agreement in the United States.[47] So insistent have we been in our blame of the Russians for the failures of disarmament negotiations that we have not faced the fact that international agreements to disarm will be reciprocal, that they will entail important limitations on the United States, that they may require complex and intrusive foreign or international institutions for inspection and enforcement in this country.

The problems which have to be faced are institutional and constitutional. Fortunately, assuming that the President and the Senate favor the agreement, and that both houses of Congress are prepared to implement it, disarmament agreements, in their major outlines, should raise no major legal difficulties. Significantly, the constitutional problems are made easy because prohibitions, limitations, obligations, of a foreseeable agreement would apply primarily to the United States Government. The U.S. Government has no "rights" under the Constitution: it can accept limitations on its activities, including limitations on the establishment of its armies, on the possession of weapons; it can destroy or give away its property, including everything in its arsenal. It can discharge every soldier, destroy every rifle, give away every missile or airplane.

If a disarmament agreement should include prohibitions and limitations applicable to private persons and corporations, these too would raise no difficulties. Congress could forbid the manufacture of weapons or their possession, surely in implementation of a disarmament treaty. The United States could order the confiscation of existing weapons, and it is not wholly clear that there would be a Constitutional obligation to compensate industry or individuals for their losses, although in might be politic to do so.[48] Private owners of patents for armaments also have no constitutional right to exploit them. Perhaps, if an agreement goes so far as to limit or regulate private scientists and private scientific

37

research, one may have to face claims of liberty under the due process clause and perhaps under the First Amendment, but even these freedoms are probably subject to some limitation "for reasons that are exigent and obviously compelling."[49] Precedent already exists in the Atomic Energy Act for the regulation of research, for requiring disclosures of the fruits of research, for appropriation of these fruits by the United States.

The difficult problems, then, are not in the substantive limitations of any foreseeable disarmament agreement. They are rather in the means and machinery for their implementation and enforcement, in that very "inspection" that the United States so earnestly seeks in the Soviet Union. Here too the area of difficulty is limited because much of the inspection will apply to facilities of the Government of the United States. The United States has no right to be secure against unreasonable searches and seizures; it has no privilege not to be compelled to be a witness against itself. The United States may agree to provide any reports on the production of weapons or materials, on the numbers and whereabouts of armaments or troops. The United States could agree to aerial inspection. It could agree to allow foreign international inspectors, at any time, into any government office or installation, to examine any document or article and to rummage at will. The United States could authorize inspectors to interrogate any federal official or former official, and could require these officials to make available any official documents or to testify about their official activities.

The problems begin when inspection and interrogation hit the private citizen. Mill owners and scientists, doctors and mine foremen would have information concerning arms and materials which might be the subject of a disarmament agreement. And if the treaty is implemented by federal criminal laws, answers to some interrogations might be within the privilege against self-incrimination (even if the witness is in fact innocent of any crime). It may take an immunity statute to meet the privilege and keep international interrogation effective.

Less easily resolved are difficulties raised by the right against unreasonable search and seizure. This right is enjoyed by corporations as well as individuals, by commercial enterprise as well as private home. Would disarmament inspection constitute "search"?[50] If so, is it "unreasonable," or might it be unreasonable in some circumstances? Of course, if inspectors were required to obtain warrants from an American court the constitutional questions might disappear. But that would hardly be feasible, as indeed we would not agree that American or international inspectors in Russia should require a warrant from a Soviet court. Effective inspection, moreover, might require the "spot-check" where there is no probable cause to support a warrant. Again, the difficulties might be reduced if inspection were limited to "regulated industry," say, acknowledged manufacturers of weapons or materials who are inspected to enforce limitations on the amounts or kinds manufactured. It is more difficult, constitutionally, if the inspectors are entitled to inspect a button factory to determine that it is indeed a button factory, not a cover for something forbidden. It is more difficult still if inspectors wish to inspect a farmer's silo to be sure it is not covering a missile site; or a house, to be sure that the guest bathroom is not in fact a small laboratory for the testing or manufacture of cultures for germ warfare.

These are among the questions for lawyers to consider. They will have to decide what the Constitution requires and whether the Constitution has to be amended. If so, they may have views too as to whether disarmament is important enough to warrant important incursions into traditional liberties. They will wish to be sure too that the dangers are realistic, the intrusions sufficiently probable and acute to raise the warning flags of the Constitution.

Lawyers will also help draft and apply any legislation implementing a treaty. Legislation might include changes in regulation of government security and classification; prohibition or regulation of the armaments industry; criminal laws to implement the treaty; privileges and facilities for the inspectorate.[51] Legislation should include, too, protection of citizens against abuse of the inspection system, perhaps compensation for property destroyed, for damage done by low overflights by aerial inspectors, for compromise of trade secrets. And Congress might see fit to enact legislation of a very different kind: standby legislation for the eventuality that breach of the agreement by others might compel the United States to consider itself free of the agreement and proceed to take steps in self-defense.

The lawyer will be involved, too, in measures to prevent or alleviate economic dislocations due to disarmament. There seems to be a deep if latent concern that disarmament would bring economic depression, and the fears and pressures that are stirred today whenever a defense contract is terminated suggest that such fears may not be easy to allay. In fact, studies by economists have indicated that the problem is not serious.[52] In the early stages, disarmament may well involve few and minimal reductions; in fact, inspection and administration of disarmament may, at the start, cost substantially more than the saving on disarmament.[53] In any event, the process will surely be gradual, allowing considerable time to reconvert factories or industries and personnel to peaceful pursuits. What is clear, on the other hand, is that such relocations and reconversions will require planning, legislation and administration. It is to be hoped that, in connection with any proposals seriously in negotiation, there would be serious planning and draft legislation to deal with any disturbing economic consequences.

III. THE LAWYER IN THE COMMUNITY [54]

There is yet another role for the lawyer in relation to the complexities of disarmament and foreign policy. The lawyer is often looked to for guidance by fellow citizens, and in large measure he helps direct the attitudes of the citizen with respect to important issues of national policy. In regard to disarmament he will find that in the community there persist, simultaneously, consistent support for disarmament efforts along with skepticism and aparthy about attempts to achieve it. But both interest and skepticism are hardly based on knowledge. Despite the now-available literature, the citizen tends to accept his ignorance about disarmament, and to leave decision to the experts, or to "Washington." And Washington, too, including his representatives in Congress, tends to leave it to the experts. The result is that issues vital to the nation are determined by the views or the whims of a few men.

What is even more unfortunate, it is not always clear that we are leaving to experts questions that are in the domain of their expertise. The citizen often does not see, and the expert himself at times fails to see, the limited jurisdiction of the expert's expertise, and the limits of his knowledge even within his domain. For after all the experts are through and their testimony is in, their conflicts noted and evaluated, the ultimate decisions are political and must be made by those in whom political power ultimately resides. Ultimately it is the citizen and his political leaders who must decide what risks are worth taking, which risks are less desirable than others, which of conflicting policies to pursue, what costs to assume. It requires expert advice, but it is not a "technical" question,

40

to determine how intense an effort should be made by the United States to make progress toward arms control; how much money, resources, energy should be devoted to the arms race, how much, for example, to research to improve the opportunities for arms control. It is a political question, calling for advice of a different kind of expert, how the activity of the government should be organized to develop and carry out disarmament policy and to assure that other political, military and technical activities of the government support the agreed policy rather than hamper it. Even in details of arms control policy, the scientists and the military, for example, can estimate the importance of continuing nuclear testing to our future preparedness; they may even guess intelligently —although apparently they are not in agreement[55]—whether, if both the United States and the Soviet Union continue testing, the United States will be better off than if neither side tests. It is a political judgment whether such advantage to the United States, if it exists, is more important than the political benefits that might flow from a test ban. Ultimately, it is even a political and psychological question, not strictly a military or a "technical" one, whether a particular inspection system affords adequate confidence of Soviet compliance; or the ultimate question—whether deterrence will work, how much we can rely on it, what alternatives—including disarmament—we might pursue.

The lawyer may also have to exercise a different leadership in disarmament. Long failure and frustration have bred skepticism and suspicion. Disarmament may have become a discredited policy. With fear and distrust of the Soviet Union long and deeply embedded, it may be difficult to obtain congressional and public support for any agreement, even if the Executive should conclude that it is in the national interest.[56] The move from security through armaments alone to enhanced security through some disarmament or arms control may require special measures to re-educate not only some military leaders, but also Congress and the public. They may have to be shown that confidence in arms may not be as warranted as we wish to believe, confidence in arms control may be more warranted than we have come to believe. They may have to be shown—if the government decides to conclude a particular agreement—that arms control, in general or in a particular form, is better for United States security and for other national interests; that the presumptions are not necessarily in favor of continued arms race rather than of some agreement; that a particular agree-

41

ment will not give the Soviet Union any lopsided advantages; that to insist on more inspection than is needed may needlessly deprive the United States of an agreement which is in our national interests.[57] Lawyers may have to show, too, that an agreement will not involve serious, unwarranted intrusions into our traditional ways; that it will be less expensive than armament, yet will not have a long term harmful impact on the economy; that it will bar military but permit scientific peaceful technological progress.

* * *

Disarmament is a problem for the lawyer—as citizen, as lawyer, as communal leader. It is not his task alone. Neither can he wholly turn from it. With others he must help assure national policies on a vital issue which promote the nation's interests in a world he can contemplate with equanimity, perhaps with hope.

PART TWO
THE FORUM

THE FORUM: A SUMMARY OF THE PROCEEDINGS*

I. DISARMAMENT: CONTEXT AND PROSPECT

Professor HENKIN introduced the subject by pointing out that the kind of issues which disarmament raises are, for the most part, not yet legal. It has been suggested, he observed, that the progress of civilization in international society may be characterized as transforming issues settled by force to issues settled by politics or diplomacy, and then transforming political issues to legal ones. Disarmament does not yet involve legal issues in the same sense as the postwar disputes relating to Berlin, or the Congo, or even Cuba—the subjects of the previous Forums.

Professor HENKIN centered his discussion on three principal questions:

First, what has been going on, in regard to disarmament, since the Second World War?

Second, why have we been negotiating for 17 years and not gotten anywhere?

Third, what is going to happen? ..

A. *Seventeen Years of Failure*

In reply to the first question, "What has been achieved?" to most people the answer is, "Nothing." Professor HENKIN pointed out that this may be exaggeration because the negotiations, though they have not succeeded, have had international effects. One obvious example is the moratorium on tests, which grew out of the negotiations although there was no formal agreement. The effects of disarmament negotiations on international politics are hard to identify and assess, but students of these problems are confident that there are important consequences, for example on armament policies and planning.

Perhaps before we ask why we have been negotiating for 17 years and not gotten anywhere, we should ask why the two big

---

* Prepared by Robert M. Pennoyer, Esq. of the New York Bar.

powers, with conflicting interests and policies, heavily armed and conducting an arms race in the most deadly weapons ever known, have continued to negotiate about disarmament. Behind these two questions lie other, older questions which were much debated during the period between the two World Wars: "Do armaments cause political tensions, or is it political tensions which cause arms races?" Or stated differently, must one have a settlement of political differences before there can be disarmament, or must one have some reduction in armaments before one can expect political settlements?

To understand the postwar disarmament picture, continued Professor HENKIN, one must seek to understand the relationship of political tensions to armaments and to the efforts to achieve disarmament. Ovbiously, disarmament is a possible national policy. Agreed disarmament between two nations would be an alternative to an uncontrolled arms race without any agreement. The question we ought to ask ourselves first therefore is, why do nations arm? If we develop some answers, we might then ask whether nations might not achieve their purposes as well or better if they agreed to disarm.

In pursuit of their national policies, the United States and the Soviet Union have been building armaments since World War II. The respective armaments reflect their competitive interests stemming from the basic confrontation between East and West. Soviet armaments respond to Russia's fears for its security, as well as the expansionist aims which we believe it has. The armaments of the West serve the needs of our security and our determination to contain Communism.

Wouldn't it be possible, Professor HENKIN asked, to achieve security by disarmament and to limit the competition of the cold war to the political and economic spheres? Those who "suggest that you can have a comprehensive disarmament scheme within the framework of the cold war must assume that, though the Soviet Union will continue to wish to export communism and the United States will continue to wish to contain it, both sides can do this as well, and less dangerously and less expensively, in a disarmed state. Even on this assumption, our side, at least, has not been confident that the Soviet Union is, in fact, willing to conduct this competition by political and economic means. We are not sure that, although the Russians say general and complete dis-

46

armament, they are really prepared to eschew arms. This, of course, gets us into the problem of inspection, among others, and its leads to the suggestion that there can be no disarmament if you don't have inspection." And the Russians have resisted inspection. Some forms of disarmament, moreover, cannot be effectively inspected.

But the problem of inspection, said Professor HENKIN, is not enough to explain the total failure of negotiations. The fact is that the pressures to disarm have not been great enough. "One must conclude, on the basis of seventeen years of frustration, that the fear of war, the terrible dangers inherent in the so-called balance of terror, the pressures of world opinion concentrated in repeated resolutions in the U.N. and elsewhere, the economic benefits which one might expect in the long run from a comprehensive disarmament system, just don't seem to be enough to overcome whatever reasons both sides have had for arming. Above all, perhaps, it seems that we are not sufficiently afraid of war. The Russians have certainly never acted as though they are afraid of war; and although we don't trust the Russians and we are afraid of what they might do, we don't really act as though we are afraid of war. In addition, we have a confidence in the weapons we have, perhaps more than is wholly justified; inevitably, you feel better when you have a big arsenal. Also we seem to be comfortable or confident about the world we live in, and we know what the world is like with the arms race, but we don't know what the world might be like when disarmament has started, and we prefer the known fears to the uncertain ones." This may help explain, if anything can, why the two sides have not been eager to disarm. That despite this lack of eagerness both sides have continued to negotiate may have a number of explanations, as suggested in the working paper.

B. *The Modest Promises of Disarmament*

Still, Professor HENKIN went on to say, both sides in the cold war must sense that the present situation is too dangerous and that we might be able to do a little something to increase the likelihood that there will be no holocaust. This raises the final question: What will happen in the future? Professor HENKIN suggested that while foretelling the future is risky business, one can indicate some limits on what may happen with a good degree of confidence. These are discussed in his working paper as the modest promises of disarmament.

As long as the Russians pursue their expansionist policies and we resist as we have, the chances of major disarmament seem very small. Certainly at the beginning, nothing radical is likely to happen. The hope for international agreement depends on finding some areas of common interest. It is wrong, empasized Professor HENKIN, to assume that we and the Russians have no common interests, even during cold war. If we consider what might be such common interests one can at least identify the subjects on which agreement is possible in the early stages.

As a result of recent studies there is reason to believe that a number of possible agreements of common interest need not raise serious problems of inspection. Some agreements can be readily monitored, either unilaterally by external means, or with minimal penetration into Soviet (and American) society. The test ban, for example. That is not disarmament, but it may suggest a willingness to put an end, in particular, to research and development of even more terrible new weapons.

There are other common interests. Since neither we nor the Russians want an all-out war, there may be a common interest in trying to reduce the danger of such a war. The "hot line" proposal—to install a direct line of communication between Moscow and the White House to reduce the likelihood of unwanted wars— has been accepted in principle by the Russians. It, too, raises no inspection problems. Other examples include the common interest in preventing the spread of nuclear weapons to other countries. The Soviets apparently do not wish the Chinese to have such weapons, and we do not wish the Germans and French to have them.

In reply to a question from the floor, Professor HENKIN stated that to come to formal agreement on such a policy would present problems—such as how it could be monitored. On the other hand, if we are persuaded that there is this common interest we need not be too worried about the Russians violating it and they need not be too worried about our violating it. Of course, despite any such agreement Communist China and one or two other countries might try to develop nuclear weapons without outside assistance from the Big Powers. That is a difficult, slow and expensive process, and for the near future it is unlikely that any major nuclear weapons programs could develop in any other country without outside assistance.

If there is a desire to reduce tension, Professor HENKIN observed, first steps in disarmament are an easier place to begin than, say, Berlin. Negotiations in disarmament are already in progress, agreements could be modest and reciprocal. Berlin, on the other hand, involves a complex situation and there we and the Russians have a direct physical confrontation. In disarmament, the most promising approach may be what Mr. Thomas Schelling, one of the most thoughtful writers about disarmament, calls the tacit agreement. We have known such agreements in the past. For example, we did not bomb across the Yalu River in Korea and the Chinese Communists did not bomb Japan. This kind of agreement is possible in the disarmament field and some say that such an agreement is already in effect with respect to not spreading nuclear weapons to other countries. The Russians did not help the Chinese as far as we can tell in any appreciable way, and we have been unwilling to help the French or the Germans. Of course, said Professor HENKIN, "tacit agreements have a great advantage. You don't have to draft and negotiate them. Generally they are in areas where there is no problem of inspection. You don't need any complicated organizations to enforce them. In addition, it is easier for people to get into them, because they don't have to go through the formalities of approval and ratification; often they require only inaction which can be more easily achieved both in Washington and in Moscow. And you don't have ever to admit that the agreement exists. On the other hand, it is also easy to get out of. You just walk out of it, recognizing that if you do, the other side may do the same."

Continuing his discussion of tacit agreements, Professor HENKIN said that an important kind of "agreement" in which we are now engaged lies in the recognition that if we double our arms budget the Russians would do the same. In that sense we have a tacit agreement not to increase our armament expenditures beyond certain limits. In the same way, if one side started to tone down its weapons program, the other side might respond. The same principle applies to our effort to make clear that our intentions are totally defensive. This is not always easy to do because the same weapons can be used for both offensive and defensive purposes. But it is clear that if we engage in one type of arms program instead of another, the Russians would be more inclined to believe that we have only defensive and deterrent intentions.

Such areas of common interest may afford some basis for progress in controlling armaments. Barring some change in the cold war— because Russia fears China or for some other reason—only these limited measures might be expected. Yet, if some initial steps were taken, these could lead to important changes in the cold war, and consequent promises for more disarmament.

Concluding his remarks, Professor HENKIN observed that what he said in the discussion and in the working paper did not sound very hopeful or optimistic about disarmament. But he wished to make it clear that "those narrow areas where hope is substantial are important, that—although the test ban, for example, will not scuttle a single weapon—it is important to exploit such areas in which we and the Russians have a common interest, to prevent the spread of weapons and to try and tamp down the arms race rather than expand it. Those areas of promise deserve all the attention and effort that we can give them."

II. THE MILITARY CONTEXT

Mr. MC NAUGHTON focused his discussion on the problem of disarmament in its military context, emphasizing that he did not believe that this was the largest context. Military power is a tool, not an end. It is intended to assist the foreign policy of the United States, to protect its security.

To illustrate the military problem confronting the West, Mr. MC NAUGHTON began by asking the audience to imagine a triangle on a globe. The triangle would start at a point midway between the Diomede Islands in the straits between Siberia and Alaska. A line drawn from this point due north through the North Pole on over the globe for a distance of 5,000 miles would bring one to the Pyrenees Mountains. Starting at the same point in the Diomede Islands, another line drawn southwest for 5,000 miles would bring one to Viet Nam. To complete the triangle, one would swing a line from Viet Nam around to the Pyrenees, a distance of 7,000 miles. But for nuclear weapons, continued Mr. MC NAUGHTON, the Soviets have superior military power in that triangle. He noted that none of the area is in the Southern Hemisphere, that only a small bit is in the Western Hemisphere, and that the triangle comprises only about one half of the remaining quarter of the earth's surface.

The difference between that triangle and the area within the Iron and Bamboo Curtains constitutes the small areas about which we spend our time worrying. Most of Western Europe is inside the triangle but outside the Iron Curtain. Some areas of southeast

50

Asia and the Near East are inside the triangle but outside the Bamboo Curtain. These are the areas where the Communists would have what one might call "conventional superiority" and would have the advantage were it not for nuclear weapons. These are the "blackmail zones"—the zones within which the Sino-Soviet can exert pressure, using the threat of their superior conventional military capabilities.

Mr. MC NAUGHTON also noted three interesting enclaves. Berlin is the first. This is a place where the Soviets obviously have a military superiority but the territory is ours. The other two enclaves are Formosa and Cuba. In the case of the latter, the Communists claim it as theirs, but it is in a part of the world where we have "conventional superiority"—that is, it is not inside the triangle. As to Formosa, people express different views as to whether it is inside or outside the triangle and as to whose territory it is.

The main point is, Mr. MC NAUGHTON continued, that but for nuclear weapons there would be a situation in which the Soviets can exert a "bargaining-table intimidation" with respect to these shadow areas between the two lines. This is why the United States refers to the nuclear weapon as an "equalizer."

Nuclear superiority, said Mr. MC NAUGHTON, is needed in order to protect these shadow areas. Otherwise, the Soviets could move in and take them over. What the weapons can do in fact is not the only matter of importance. Also important is "the shadow that our nuclear capability casts on the bargaining table." If the United States is resisting some form of pressure over Berlin, the capabilities reflect themselves in the negotiations. They reflect themselves in the amount of backbone one has, the amount of backbone one's allies have, and the amount of pressure the Soviets can apply.

In reply to a question from the floor Mr. MC NAUGHTON explained that in order for the West's nuclear strength to deter Soviet aggression in Western Europe we must make our use of nuclear weapons credible to the Soviets. Under one theory, this is accomplished by maintaining a conventional capability of such magnitude that an attempt by the Soviets to overrun Western Europe would lead to large-scale fighting which in turn would escalate into a nuclear war. There are, however, other theories. At one extreme some persons abroad question the need of very much conventional power. They advocate the use of nuclear weap-

51

CARNEGIE LIBRARY
LIVINGSTONE COLLEGE
SALISBURY, N. C. 28144

ons to deter any aggression. All it takes, they say, is determination, or will. Another point of view is that the very willingness to fight a conventional war makes the Russians less willing to believe that we will use our nuclear weapons.

In reply to another question from the floor Mr. MC NAUGHTON explained that the nuclear weapons now in Germany have warheads which are kept entirely under United States custody. The warheads are kept completely separate from any other allied personnel.

A. *The Role of the Unilateral Decision*

Turning to a discussion of the risks arising from the present military confrontation, Mr. MC NAUGHTON stated that he intended to emphasize an aspect of arms control which Professor HENKIN mentioned but did not emphasize. Whereas Professor HENKIN spoke of alternative approaches to disarmament by negotiated and non-negotiated agreement, Mr. MC NAUGHTON wished to focus on the unilateral decision as a method of arms control—something of special interest to the Defense Department. This does not mean, Mr. MC NAUGHTON stressed, that the Department of Defense does not support negotiation. But it is the business of the Department of Defense to manage the armaments of the country and it is, therefore, natural that it focus on those aspects of arms control which do not require agreement on the part of anyone else and which can be managed by simple, straightforward unilateral decisions.

One example of the unilateral decision is found in the enormous amount of effort and money which the United States spends to avoid accidental or unauthorized explosion of a nuclear weapon. Not only must people who handle the weapons be carefully picked but procedures which require the cooperation of several people to set off a weapon must be established. Under procedures which we have put into effect it takes "anywhere from three to fifteen actions to get one of these things to the point where it can be used." The military sometimes complain about such restrictions on the ground that when we really want to use the weapons, we will not be able to perform in time all three or fifteen actions, as the case may be.

Related to the first area is another—the area of miscalculation. Examples of unilateral decision in this area include placing missiles on submarines and positioning missiles in underground "silos". The purpose in each case is to make missiles less vulnerable. If they are above ground, as were the Jupiter missiles in Italy and Turkey, they are vulnerable and act like "bait" for an attack. In the event of an unidentified explosion or any type of situation where tension is running very high, if such weapons are to be used they would have to be used quickly. One does not have enough time to confirm whether the weapons must be used because they could be destroyed in a few minutes. Thus, efforts to make our missiles less vulnerable contribute not only to our security but to Soviet security because the fact that the Soviets know that we are not trigger happy eases the tension and helps to avoid miscalculation.

The final area, Mr. MC NAUGHTON continued, in which one can take precautions by simple unilateral decision is to ensure command and control of weapons in order to reduce damage in the event of war. One of the primary problems is to figure out a way to stop a war if it gets started, to keep a war from escalating —for example, by choosing targets so as to avoid Soviets cities and to aim instead at Soviet weapons.

Mr. MC NAUGHTON, referring to Professor HENKIN's statement that one should avoid doing things which cause the other side to react, emphasized that one must consider the negative aspect of each action. Thus, placing missiles under ground may cause the Russians to use bigger warheads or a ground blast instead of an air blast with the resulting increase in fallout. There is a give and take here. Our efforts must be to make decisions which are somewhat tempered, and which are designed to minimize the Soviet counteraction, and to increase our net security.

Mr. MC NAUGHTON explained that he brought these points up only to show the challenge facing the Department of Defense to be sure that our weapons, strategy and research and development are re-examined with a view toward heading off the difficulties to which he referred. The Department of Defense wants to protect our interests while maintaining stability so that no one starts a war, and to the extent possible avoid aggravating the arms race.

III. THE SOVIET UNION: OBJECTIVES AND MEANS

Professor HAZARD centered his discussion on two questions: First, do the Soviet leaders want disarmament?

Second, what is the likelihood of finding a formula they and we could accept?

As to the first, Professor HAZARD said he agreed with Professor HENKIN as to the principle that must govern our answer—that disarmament can be acceptable only if it serves better or as well the purposes for which nations build and maintain armaments. The analysis in Professor HENKIN's working paper, said Professor Hazard, caught the real spirit of the Soviet position on disarmament.

The aim of expansionism is clearly present in Soviet theories. Their ideology has been based on the assumption that the Communist system is on the wave of the future. Professor HAZARD said that he saw "no lessening in this ardor," as confirmed by recent reports of the acceptance by Soviet students of the conclusion that state ownership of the means of production is the only possible way to live.

Confronted with this aim of expansionism, the point to which we have to direct our attention is the question of means. In this connection, it was very important in 1957 when Khrushchev took the position that it was no longer necessary for the achievement of Communism that there be war. Until then the Communist position had been that war was essential to the achievement of their goals. Their new position, in Professor HAZARD's opinion, is very firmly held, as attested by Khrushchev's tenacity in defending his decision against the Chinese even to the point of admitting a break which is certainly detrimental to his position around the world.

Continuing his analysis of the changes in Soviet attitudes, Professor HAZARD said that, although the Communists maintain a policy of expansionism, it is not by way of atomic holocaust. This suggests one reason why the U.S.S.R. might accept some measure of disarmament—at least atomic disarmament and control. They want to keep control on their side in their own hands and ensure that "hotheads" like the Chinese don't have the bomb or use it in some way opposed by the Russians.

Professor HAZARD also emphasized the Soviet interest in deterrent and defense. At the outset of the Soviet regime in the 1920's and 1930's, with the rise of Hitler, the Soviet Union saw itself in great peril. Today the picture is different. The Soviet Union has the power in contrast to the past, but seems to use this power not to start an atomic war but to protect itself from annihilation. Their new declaration in favor of disarmament may be related to their concern for deterrent and defense. It is possible, Professor HAZARD suggested, that the Soviet leaders called for disarmament not for propaganda effect but, more importantly, because it offers the only hope they have of remaining in power. They want to be sure that no one but the United States and Britain have the atomic bomb. They do not believe that we are going to use the bomb foolhardily, but they do not have the same confidence in the case of Castro. They would not want the Chinese to have it either, and they certainly would not want the Egyptians to have it. Above all, they would not want the Germans to have it.

Most Americans, Professor HAZARD emphasized, do not appreciate how much the Russians fear Germany. From our point of view the Germans are cut in half, they have relatively little armament, and they could not possibly hurt Russia. But the Russians believe that the Germans have a great desire for revenge, and to them the only really dangerous thing in the world is Germany. In the Russian view, the Germans are the people who must not under any circumstances get the bomb. For this, said Professor HAZARD, they would give up quite a bit.

In reply to a question from the floor Professor HAZARD said that in his view the settlement of the Berlin question is not essential to reaching an agreement on disarmament. In his opinion, Berlin to the Russians is an irritant and not a threat. The real danger from their point of view is in the Germans having the bomb. If the Russians are ever prepared to come to agreement, it is going to have to include, said Professor HAZARD, some provision on our part that the West Germans will not have nuclear weapons. By contrast, from their standpoint Berlin would be "an awfully small part of the package," although we can expect them to seek a change in its status.

Professor HAZARD turned next to a discussion of the Soviet concern that their people have more consumer goods. The Soviet Union, he said, is very much over-extended. It cannot build armaments and at the same time feed, house and clothe people as they would like to be fed, housed and clothed—particularly housed. The process of governing the Soviet Union has been seriously hampered by great shortages. If armaments could be reduced, both conventional and atomic, it would be a delight to Soviet policy makers.

There are therefore strong reasons why the U.S.S.R. would accept a disarmament plan that would keep atomic weapons in the hands of those who now have them and also head off the arms race so as to permit the U.S.S.R. to maintain its deterrent, but at a lessened cost. This would be in their interest because they would not have to fear the irrational use of nuclear weapons, and could devote more funds to the improvement of their country and to providing aid to other developing countries which they consider their entering wedge to bring Communism to the world.

There is, however, the question of control. It is to the advantage of the U.S.S.R., Professor HAZARD noted, to control the United States and its allies, particularly Germany. But what price are the Russians prepared to pay to get this control over the United States? Do they have to offer control to the United States over their own country, or can they offer a lesser price? They think they already know enough about the United States. Our democratic system, the open society which we run and are determined to preserve, make it easy for the Soviets to find out what is going on. Their agents can function more efficiently in our country than we have been able to in theirs, where we cannot move around so freely.

Since they do not have to pay a price to have a reasonably good inspection system of us, Professor HAZARD said that he doubted that the Russians would be willing to open themselves to our inspection or to the controls which we think we need. If we are to reach agreement, it must be on some basis other than a trading of inspection teams. The scientists may be moving in the direction of providing a sense of security to us without inspection teams residing in the U.S.S.R. Possibly some form of spot-check inspection would be acceptable to us. If so, said Professor HAZARD, there would be a good chance of disarmament because, for the reasons indicated, it is to the Soviets' advantage to have some measure of disarmament. If not, and it is imperative that we have on-site inspection in the U.S.S.R., he would see no chance of a significant step toward disarmament.

IV. THE ROLE OF THE UNITED STATES

A. *The Postwar Setting*

Mr. DEAN opened his remarks by saying that Professor HEN-KIN was correct in stating that nothing tangible in the way of agreement has been accomplished in 17 years of negotiation. Reviewing events since World War II, Mr. DEAN said that he believed that fundamentally nothing would have assured any kind of cooperation between what we call the Free World and the Communist world, including Communist China, in the aftermath of the war when we were struggling to rehabilitate Japan and Germany and bring about the independence of Austria. At the end of the war we reduced our forces from 12.5 million to 1.5 million men. We offered to transfer the entire control of all fissionable material and the further production of the bomb to an international agency under the supervision of the U.N. The Soviets rejected that.

We then had the Marshall Plan, and restored Europe. We had the trouble over the Suez Canal which was solved peacefully. All through this period we saw the transfer to independence of enormous numbers of people, such as India from England and Indonesia from Holland; and practically all the countries of Africa were transferred from their former rulers to independence so that, as of today, very small numbers of people are still in a colonial status.

All of this, said Mr. DEAN, has been accomplished either through negotiation with the Soviet Union, or through force of arms, or through economic aid, or through the United Nations, or through these tacit understandings to which Professor HENKIN referred.

B. *Disarmament Proposals*

We started on disarmament negotiations some 17 years ago. We have met at various times with the Soviet Union in a effort to bring about some plan of disarmament. In Mr. DEAN's personal opinion, derived from spending some 18 hours a day with them for well over two years, the Russians don't want disarmament, and they don't want a nuclear test ban treaty with any adequate inspection. As Communists they believe that it is inevitable that they will rule society—that is the law of history. They believe that we will go under and they will rule, and it is only just a question of time when that will happen. They repeat that to you, said Mr. DEAN, "day after day, hour after hour, second after second, until it becomes terribly boring." Nevertheless, he said, it seems one could "convince practically everybody in the world of the good intentions of the United States except the scholarly world of American universities. They are convinced that our government doesn't really want a nuclear test ban treaty . . ."

Mr. DEAN emphasized that this is not correct. The United States drafted a disarmament treaty which provided for the elimination of all arms and of all men in three stages, and in the third stage for the setting up of a peace force to take care of untoward events in the world under the general jurisdiction of the United Nations. Mr. DEAN also stated that in an effort to get a nuclear test ban treaty at Geneva on August 27, 1962 we had eliminated the threshold and separated the nuclear test ban treaty into two parts, one banning tests in outer space, the atmosphere and on and under water, without inspection and any control commission, and the other text banning tests underground with an appropriate commission and with adequate inspection.

In reply to a question from the floor Mr. DEAN agreed that a disarmament treaty would have to make careful provision with respect to voting by the various member states. He said that the arrangements included in the draft disarmament treaty proposed by the United States on August 18, 1962 specified the voting rights to which countries of the Free World and the Soviet Union and the non-aligned nations would be entitled.

What kind of treaty did the Soviets put in? Theirs, continued Mr. DEAN, provided that in the first 22 months, which was later extended to 24 months, the United States would have to give up every ship, every airplane, every missile and every rocket capable of carrying a nuclear warhead. We would have to give up every foreign base, and we would have to withdraw all American troops to the North American continent. That would mean that we would have to give up our security treaties, get out of the North Atlantic Treaty Organization and the Organization of American States, get our troops out of Japan and Korea, out of Formosa, out of the Philippines, out of the South-east Asia Treaty Organization countries, and give up all our foreign bases.

That would leave the United States at the end of the first stage of the Soviet proposed disarmament treaty, naked and alone on the North American continent, absolutely unable to move. If anybody like India or other victims of the Chinese asked for weapons, we couldn't deliver them.

But the Soviets, on the other hand, under their treaty would have to give up only one third of their conventional weapons in the first stage. They could still move, although at a slower pace, from Germany to the Pacific.

We have pointed this out, Mr. DEAN continued, again and

again to the Soviets. We have offered to modify our disarmament plan. We have gone into this question of manpower with them because their treaty would require us to reduce our forces to 1.7 million men, a highly intelligent calculation on their part because it would require us to bring back our troops from foreign bases which is something they devoutly wish will come about. Foreign Secretary Gromyko has made certain proposed modifications in the Soviet Disarmament Plan to carry nuclear weapons into the second stage of their plan and to lengthen it somewhat. While these changes are encouraging, we do not believe they are sufficiently realistic.

We can honestly say, emphasized Mr. DEAN, that the United States with good intent and in good faith tried to present an honest treaty which would work, and which in the third stage would completely end all armaments and all armed forces under national authority. Their plan, however, was apparently "a plan to disarm the Free World, and in their lighter moments, they had no hesitation in admitting it."

Mr. DEAN said that he agreed with Professor HAZARD that the Russians are terribly afraid of the Germans. The Germans killed 22,000,000 Russians, and practically every Russian family lost one or two. They are dreadfully afraid that even in NATO, where we point out that we have tight nuclear weapon control, somehow or other the Germans will get control of those nuclear weapons and attack Russia. This is something, Mr. DEAN continued, that we will have to face if we ever get down to brass tacks with them on a treaty.

The Russians have also insisted that the peace organization as well as the disarmament organization be ruled by three people, the so-called troika—one from the West, one from the Communist world, and one from the Neutralist world—each of whom would have the right of veto over the others. If we ever found ourselves without an army, navy or air force, or without any missiles, and relying on the peace force of the United Nations, the Russians as a member of the Security Council would have the right to veto the use of that force.

The question of whether permanent members of the Security Council should continue to have the right of veto in the United Nations over the use of peace forces is a most critical matter and one which will require the most careful study. With some 111 members in the General Assembly, which number will undoubt-

59

edly increase as further countries gain their independence, Mr. DEAN stated that he doubted that it would be favorable to have the voting authority with respect to the use or non-use of the United Nations peace force transferred to the General Assembly where, in time of crisis, the matter might become a political football.

Mr. DEAN went on to say that Deputy Foreign Minister Kuznetzov and Foreign Minister Zorin would tell him again and again that he was foolish to think about any plan which would take away from the permanent members of the Security Council the right to veto the use of the peace force because someday the United States would want to exercise that veto. This, Mr. DEAN observed, is one of the big problems to which we have never really addressed ourselves. When the United Nations was being drafted in San Francisco, we at that time thought of the Secretary General as the administrative agent of the five permanent members of the Security Council. Mr. DEAN said that he doubted whether we would want to entrust the use of that force entirely to the Secretary General since we would not know who that might be. We certainly would not want to put it in the General Assembly, with 110 members and perhaps 125 members a few years from now, on a majority vote. But if the use of the force was subject to a veto, we would be giving up our army, navy and airforce with no sure way of knowing how the peace would be kept.

Turning to the effort to get a nuclear test ban treaty, Mr. DEAN recalled that under President Eisenhower we had spent about $100,000,000 trying to figure out better ways of detecting, locating and distinguishing between a nuclear explosion and an earthquake. The motions from a natural phenomenon are much more complicated than the motions from a man-made explosion. In an earthquake there will be movements under the crust of the earth in several directions whereas in a nuclear explosion the force is outward from the center of the event. In the event of an explosion underground it can carry in any one of four directions—northeast, southwest, northwest or southeast—and it would require a barebone minimum of four detection stations to record the sounds. One probably should have more than that. Then one has to decide whether it is an earthquake or a nuclear event. If one can't tell and one decides to dig, one would have to determine the exact location. In order to be effective, the exact location must be determined with a good deal of precision before digging is commenced, or otherwise the epicenter of the explosion would never be found. It would, of course, be simpler if reconnaissance planes could be flown over the suspected territory in order to see whether there are areas of subsidence, but so far the Soviets have been unwilling to agree to such reconnaissance planes, and have been unwilling to agree to a realistic number of detection stations or to their proper equipment or manning. There are numerous problems with respect to automatic stations which will have to be resolved.

Based on our research we have offered a very realistic test ban treaty. Many people have called the number of detection stations and on-site inspections concessions but, said Mr. DEAN, a better way to put it is that the United States has tried to make the treaty more workable, to reduce the cost, and really to stop further nuclear testing.

Later in the discussion Professor HENKIN, recalling Mr. DEAN'S remark that we can convince everybody except the scholarly world of American universities of the good intentions of the United States, observed that there is a difference between saying that the United States doesn't really desire any disarmament and saying that we often advance proposals which we know are unacceptable to the Russians. The latter is surely true. For example, the first stage of the United States' draft treaty would require substantial inspection within the Soviet Union. Although we are sincere in asking for it, as Professor HAZARD has pointed out the Russians cannot accept it. It is important to keep in mind, Professor HENKIN observed, that the disarmament proposals of both the United States and Russia are negotiating positions. If there is to be substantial hope for some start in disarmament, it may be necessary to pick some particular weapon or objective the control of which does not require inspection, does not endanger our position, and is in our common interest with Russia.

In the case of the test ban, for example, we are willing, Professor HENKIN said, to have atmospheric tests banned without any inspection system whatsoever because we are able to monitor them unilaterally. Similarly, although he believed that our draft treaty contains bona fide proposals, they are not likely to be accepted as they are. We might consider, in addition, other possible first steps which don't require much inspection and which seem to offer more hope of agreement. Agreement on such first steps may lead to agreement in other areas. It is noteworthy, concluded Professor HENKIN, that the Russians have said that they would accept two or three inspections. This is quite a step for them, and the papers lead one to believe that we would agree, all of which suggests that something might yet be possible.

Mr. DEAN continued the discussion by asking why we want to stop further nuclear testing. If it is done in the atmosphere, it causes radioactive debris, and may possibly affect generations of children yet unborn. By testing, a country can advance its nuclear discoveries. If the big powers test, the small powers are going to test. Whatever the reasons, whether pressure from the Chinese Communists or internal pressures in the Soviet Union, or whether they are still terribly worried because of their discovery at the time of the Cuban crisis that we had intercontinental ballistic missile superiority over them, one thing is abundantly clear; as of the present time the Russians don't want a nuclear test ban treaty which would incorporate realistic controls. They don't want to go on discussing disarmament on any kind of realistic basis, but there will probably be further progress on the mutual stationing of observers and as how to prevent surprise attack and, possibly, on a limited number of other agreements.

In reply to a question from the floor, Mr. DEAN remarked that something is going on in Russia today. Khrushchev is still 100% in control, but his denunciation of Stalin at the twentieth Party Congress in 1956 and, during this past year, his attacks on modern art and the more advanced intellectual writers may indicate a change in Khrushchev himself. What was he doing at the time he was Stalin's deputy? Why didn't he speak out then?

There is great trouble inside the Soviet Union today. The Communists are troubled because the so-called intellectual youth is not as interested in Communism as their fathers or grandfathers were. They do not have as much of a hold on the Eastern satellites and they are troubled by their failures in Iraq and the Congo. Mr. DEAN does not mean, he said, that they are going to let up on their efforts to bring about world communism and end the ideological warfare. They are still dedicated Communists, and they still believe that ultimately Communism will dominate the world. As Premier Khrushchev himself has said, when he talks about peaceful coexistence he is not abandoning subversion, infiltration or wars of national independence.

In reply to another question from the floor Mr. DEAN commented on the changes he had observed in the Russians' negotiating position and techniques. The Communists who do the negotiating, emphasized Mr. DEAN, are carefully selected and very able, intelligent and hard working. They have very explicit instructions and they are reluctant to recommend any change in these instructions. As a result they tend to say the same thing over and over again with dreary repetition. However, Mr. DEAN has been able to detect changes. In the spring of 1961 he thought he could detect their desire to renew testing because they no longer seemed really interested in negotiating realistically. As a result it did not come as too great a surprise when they announced they would do so in September 1961. Mr. DEAN also believes, he said, that their rift with the Chinese has brought a change. Several Russians have directly admitted to him that there is little or no possibility of their agreeing to anything until they know where they stand with the Chinese Communists.

Why don't we get up and come home?

"The fact of the matter is," said Mr. DEAN, "if we don't somehow or other reduce the risks through continuous negotiations and by creative imagination and by constantly trying to make these things workable, all of humanity is faced with the fact that, either by accident or by surprise or even by design, hundreds of millions of our citizens or other citizens could be killed and entire cities destroyed in a matter of seconds. To many people it is intolerable that we continue to talk when there is no progress being made. But what is the alternative? The alternative is to walk out and to allow each side to continue to go about testing, spewing out the radioactive debris in the atmosphere, and for all of humanity to be subject to this possible catastrophe."

V. DISARMAMENT AND OTHER NATIONS

Mr. DEAN concluded his remarks by saying that there are hundreds of millions of people who are truly independent, who have no armaments, but who want nuclear testing stopped. He has heard it facetiously asked, "Well, how many divisions do they have?" The answer is "None." But, said Mr. DEAN, he doesn't "believe that the United States, as a great moral leader and leader in the world, can afford to say to those people that their entire opinions or their lives or the lives of their children will be disregarded by the United States in its policy, because they have no divisions. This is a tough thing that the United States faces, because I can't see any immediate prospect of getting an overall agreement. At the same time, I can't see any clear-cut way whereby the United States can refuse to continue negotiations." Mr. DEAN thought that in the course of the negotiations with the Russians, because of their ideological struggle with the Chinese and changes inside the Soviet Union, there will be times when negotiations will be set back by an exceedingly tough attitude on the part of the Soviets. While we must under no circumstances make unrealistic concessions or indulge in a state of euphoria with respect to our relations with the Soviets, we must not be discouraged in our attempts to bring the Soviets back into the stream of western civilization, but this will be a long and hard road.

Mr. DEAN'S discussion of the treaty proposals lead to a question from the floor as to how we would reach agreement on general disarmament without the agreement of France and Communist China.

Mr. DEAN recalled that to meet a point raised by the Soviet Union, the United States' draft treaty had been changed to provide that the United States and Russia would complete Stage One— that is, the reduction of manpower and both conventional and nuclear weapons—without Communist China becoming a party, but that China would have to become a party before Stage Two went into effect. Mr. DEAN noted that India had thought this was a wonderful provision until it was attacked by China, but now took the position it would wish to have China a party to the treaty before Stage One went into effect.

Commenting on the same point, Professor HENKIN said that by definition there could be no general agreement without France and China. The fissures in both camps, he explained, although differing in degree and quality, are relevant to the disarmament problem. France's desire to go it alone probably makes the Russians more reluctant to agree to disarm as they wait to see what will happen to the Western Alliance.

The Russians' own troubles with China may have two different kinds of effects. On the one hand, if the Russians have serious differences with the Chinese, they are not going to give up nuclear weapons which they would want to keep facing Peiping instead of us. On the other hand it may make it possible for them to enter into other kinds of agreements without being concerned about the attitude of the Chinese. But such differences do make general disarmament impossible. On the other hand, France has made it clear that she would go along with general and complete disarmament and with disarmament of various types; but she will not go along with a test ban. She does not want to let the two giants freeze their superiority and leave her out.

As to China, Professor HENKIN continued, we have always assumed that Russia could deliver the Chinese signature to an agreement, and we have felt that we would have to insist on it—because we would also want inspection in China to be sure that the Russians do not use China for testing in violation of a test ban. If we believe that the rift between Russia and China is serious and that the Russians would be unable to deliver a Chinese signature, we also need not be afraid that the Russians would use China to violate the agreement. There are a number of subjects on which we would be content with some kind of agreement with the Russians alone. The test ban might be one such agreement. Even if China and France do not agree to a test ban, agreement by Russia and the United States alone would not only turn the head of the arms race and hamper further development of terrible new weapons, but would also help prevent the spread of nuclear weapons to many countries regardless of what France and China do.

If one talks about major disarmament on a comprehensive scale, on the other hand, there are many other countries, said Professor HENKIN, which have blithely urged and voted for resolutions in the United Nations favoring disarmament, having in mind the United States and Russia and directed to getting rid of the big weapons. If the time came to ask Indonesia, Pakistan, Egypt, Israel, and others to put their own weapons on the table, they might have other thoughts and the issues of disarmament would be much more complicated.

VI. THE LAWYER'S ROLE

Professor HENKIN next turned to a discussion of disarmament issues which are of particular interest to the legal profession. Many of these issues are new manifestations of old problems. There are the problems of writing international agreements and getting states to comply with them. Lawyers will have to think of less radical suggestions than exchanging hostages. This gets into the question of organizing inspection, and the problem of enforcement in an international community which is not equipped for major sanctions. Then there is the problem of how to settle disputes. Whether or not a court could be used would depend in some measure on how quickly it could act. For many disputes the judicial process would not be appropriate.

Finally, the American lawyer ought particularly to be interested in the domestic problems—the great constitutional and other questions which would arise if the United States entered into an agreement and began to apply it in the United States. Can Russian inspectors knock at my door and say, "We wish to see whether germ warfare cultures are being made in the basement of your house?" How would one apply constitutional provisions with respect to search and seizure, or the privilege against self-incrimination? How does the businessman protect his trade secrets? Because we have never been close enough to a disarmament agreement, the American lawyer has not paid enough attention to these problems. Even a test ban—which sometimes looks quite close— might involve some of these questions, if the Russians wanted on-site inspection in the United States. It is important to study these questions. If we ever come close to agreement some people in the United States who, from the best of motives, are opposed to an agreement, might raise these constitutional points as additional objections.

In many ways the lawyer's most important role with regard to disarmament is that he—especially his voice in an organization like The Association of the Bar of the City of New York—can contribute to reason and order, to help keep what is relevant foremost in public debate, to assure that issues are decided on their merits rather than on something else. The lawyer will help to decide whether we can maintain our tradition of civilian control over the military and—equally or more important—political control over the experts, whether they are military or otherwise. It might be useful to cross-examine those who say we need more inspection, to determine whether there is anything to the belief that they are demanding unnecessary inspections because they don't really want an agreement—just as we have always accused the Russians of refusing inspections which are necessary because they don't want an agreement.

As his final comment on this point, Professor HENKIN said that there will be other kinds of fears that lawyers will have to help clear away, such as fear for the economy. Everyone is familiar with the fuss that is made when a small defense contract in a particular area is about to be terminated. Fortunately studies have been made which confirm that our economy does not require armaments to survive.

Concluding the discussion of the lawyer's role in disarmament, Mr. MC NAUGHTON stressed the lawyer's obligation to assist in educating people that the present East-West arms race is really dangerous. This point is awfully hard to get across, but in Mr. MC NAUGHTON'S view, the main job of education has to be accomplished now.

Appendix A

HIGHLIGHTS OF DISARMAMENT EFFORTS, 1945-1963

1945

December	26	Moscow Declaration of Foreign Ministers. US-UK-USSR agreed to sponsor General Assembly Resolution recommending creation of U.N. Commission on Atomic Energy

1946

January	24	U.N. General Assembly created Atomic Energy Commission
June	14	Bernard M. Baruch, in U.N. Atomic Energy Commission, presented United States plan for control of atomic energy based on the Acheson-Lilienthal Report
June-July		Soviet Union rejected U.S. proposals
August	1	United States Atomic Energy Control Act (McMahon Act) became effective
December	30	U.N. Atomic Energy Commission approved essential principles of U.S. plan for control of atomic energy calling for an International Atomic Development Authority

1947

February	13	U.N. Security Council established Commission for Conventional Armaments

1948

March	30	Control Committee of U.N. Atomic Energy Commission admitted failure and adjourned indefinitely
August	12	U.N. Commission for Conventional Armaments recommended principles for system of regulating and reducing armaments and armed forces

November	4	U.N. General Assembly approved plan of U.N. Atomic Energy Commission based upon United States proposals

1949

July	29	U.N. Atomic Energy Commission suspended work indefinitely
September	23	President Truman announced that an atomic explosion had taken place in the U.S.S.R.
October	11	Soviet Union vetoed proposal for verified census of world's non atomic armaments and armed forces
December	15	U.N. General Assembly approved proposals formulated by the Commission for Conventional Armaments

1950

March	19	Communist-sponsored World Congress of Partisans of Peace adopted "Stockholm Resolution" to ban atomic weapons
June	25	Communist forces invaded South Korea

1951

July	10	Negotiations for an armistice in Korea began

1952

January	11	U.N. General Assembly established single Disarmament Commission to replace Atomic Energy Commission and Commission for Conventional Armaments
April-August		Western proposals for disclosure and verification of forces and armaments and for numerical limitations debated and rejected by U.S.S.R.
October	3	United Kingdom detonated its first atomic device
November	1	United States tested first hydrogen bomb at Eniwetok

1953

July	27	Korean Armistice
August	20	Soviet Government announced it had tested hydrogen bomb

70

| December | 8 | President Eisenhower, in speech before U.N. General Assembly, proposed "Atoms for Peace" plan for international development of peaceful uses of atomic energy |

1954

April	19	Disarmament Comission established five power subcommittee to seek in private solution to disarmament problem
May-June		Disarmament Subcommittee held "secret sessions" in New York and London
November	4	U.N. General Assembly called for new attempt to reach East-West agreement on disarmament and prohibition of nuclear weapons

1955

March	19	President Eisenhower created post of Special Assistant to the President on Disarmament
April	24	Bandung Conference of Asian and African countries urged all states to cooperate in bringing about reduction of armaments and elimination of nuclear weapons under effective international control
May	10	Soviet Union proposal in Disarmament Commission called for international control agency with international inspectorate, including provision for "control posts in big ports, railway junctions, motor roads and airdromes"
July	18	Four Power Summit Conference opened, focusing largely on disarmament
July	21	President Eisenhower presented "open skies" proposal
July	25	United States Senate established Subcommittee of Foreign Relations Committee to "study proposals (for) disarmament and the control of weapons of mass destruction"
September	6	In U.N. Disarmament Commission Subcommittee, U.S. representative placed reservation on all previous U.S. disarmament positions
October-November		Foreign Ministers of the United States, United Kingdom, France, and the U.S.S.R. convened at Geneva, adjourned without agreement
December	3	U.N. General Assembly adopted resolution to

71

establish an International Committee on Peaceful Uses of Atomic Energy

U.N. General Assembly unanimously voted to establish 15-member scientific committee to collect, evaluate and disseminate information on effects of atomic radiation

December	Russia rejected U.S. "open skies" plan

1956-1957

March 1956- September 1957	Extensive negotiations in U.N. Disarmament Subcommittee, ended in deadlock

1956

September	11	Marshal Bulganin proposed to President Eisenhower agreement for cessation of nuclear tests

1957

May	15	United Kingdom exploded its first hydrogen weapon
June-August		U.N. Disarmament Subcommittee discussed proposals for cessation of tests
October	4	Sputnik launched
October	15	Soviet Union agreed to aid Communist China to develop atomic weapons
November	19	Disarmament Commission enlarged by U.N. General Assembly. Soviet Union announced refusal to participate in future negotiations of Disarmament Commission
December		Premier Bulganin and President Eisenhower exchanged correspondence reopening disarmament discussions

1958

March	31	Soviet Union announced discontinuance of testing for six months, to be continued if other nations refrained from testing
July-August		Geneva conference of experts on technical problems of test ban
October	31	Tripartite negotiations on test ban commenced with voluntary moratorium on testing
November		Experts' conference for study of problem of surprise attack

Test ban conference negotiated on treaty provisions but failed to reach agreement on impartial inspection agency or on amount of inspection

1959

June	20	U.S.S.R. abrogated its agreement to help Communist China to develop atomic weapons
August		Meeting of Foreign Ministers of United States, U.K., France and U.S.S.R. agreed on procedures for resuming general disarmament negotiations and established Ten Power Disarmament Committee
September	18	Premier Khrushchev presented to General Assembly proposal for General and Complete Disarmament

1960

February	13	France tested its first atomic weapon
March-April		Ten Power Disarmament Conference convened; Western delegates turned down Soviet proposal for General and Complete Disarmament
May	1	American U-2 plane crashed on Soviet territory
May		Summit Meeting in Paris
June	27	Soviet delegation walked out of Ten Power Conference

1961

March	21	Three-power test ban talks resumed after long recess
June-September		Bilateral talks between McCloy and Zorin led to American-Soviet statement of agreed disarmament principles
September	1	Soviet Union resumed nuclear testing
September	3	President Kennedy and Prime Minister Macmillan proposed that three nuclear powers agree at once not to conduct atmospheric tests
September	5	United States announced plans to resume testing
September	9	Soviet Union rejected proposal for ban on atmospheric tests only

September	25	President Kennedy submitted to General Assembly a program for "General and Complete Disarmament in a Peaceful World"
September	26	Congress established the United States Arms Control and Disarmament Agency
November	27	U.S.S.R. proposed test ban monitored by "national detection systems" only
December	20	General Assembly approved Soviet Union-United States sponsored resolution creating an 18-Nation Disarmament Committee

1962

January	16	Western powers rejected Soviet proposal for test ban monitored only by national detection systems, and proposed sending test ban question to 18-Nation Disarmament Committee
March		18-Nation Disarmament Committee began deliberations and created subcommittee on nuclear tests
April	18	United States presented to 18-Nation Disarmament Committee "Outline of Basic Provisions of a Treaty on General and Complete Disarmament in a Peaceful World"
April	25	United States resumed nuclear testing in air
December	19	Premier Khrushchev in letter to President Kennedy expressed willingness to accept test ban with three international "on-site" inspections per year

1963

January		Tripartite Discussions on Test Ban failed to achieve agreement on minimum number of "on-site" inspections
February		Republicans in Congress attacked Kennedy Administration for willingness to accept fewer on-site inspections
February	12	18-Nation Conference reconvened
March		Further tests conducted by France in the Sahara
April	5	Soviet Representative at 18-Nation Disarmament Committee accepted in principle United States proposal for direct Washington-Moscow communication system

Appendix B

On August 5, 1963 the governments of the United States, the United Kingdom and the U.S.S.R. signed a treaty banning nuclear weapons tests in the atmosphere, in outer space and underwater. Although this action followed the Hammarskjöld Forum on Disarmament by some three months, the text of the treaty is set forth below because of its relevance to the issues discussed at the Forum.

TREATY

The Governments of the United States of America, the United Kingdom of Great Britain and Northern Ireland, and the Union of Soviet Socialist Republics, hereinafter referred to as the "Original Parties",

Proclaiming as their principal aim the speediest possible achievement of an agreement on general and complete disarmament under strict international control in accordance with the objectives of the United Nations which would put an end to the armaments race and eliminate the incentive to the production and testing of all kinds of weapons, including nuclear weapons,

Seeking to achieve the discontinuance of all test explosions of nuclear weapons for all time, determined to continue negotiations to this end, and desiring to put an end to the contamination of man's environment by radioactive substances,

Have agreed as follows:

ARTICLE I

1. Each of the Parties to this Treaty undertakes to prohibit, to prevent, and not to carry out any nuclear weapon test explosion, or any other nuclear explosion, at any place under its jurisdiction or control:

(a) in the atmosphere; beyond its limits, including outer space; or underwater, including territorial waters or high seas; or

(b) in any other environment if such explosion causes radioactive debris to be present outside the territorial limits of the State under whose jurisdiction or control such explosion is conducted. It is understood in this connection that the provisions of this subparagraph are without prejudice to the conclusion of a treaty resulting in the permanent banning of all nuclear test explosions, including all such explosions underground, the conclusion of which, as the Parties have stated in the Preamble to this Treaty, they seek to achieve.

2. Each of the Parties to this Treaty undertakes furthermore to

75

refrain from causing, encouraging, or in any way participating in, the carrying out of any nuclear weapon test explosion, or any other nuclear explosion, anywhere which would take place in any of the environments described, or have the effect referred to, in paragraph 1 of this Article.

ARTICLE II

1. Any Party may propose amendments to this Treaty. The text of any proposed amendment shall be submitted to the Depositary Governments which shall circulate it to all Parties to this Treaty. Thereafter, if requested to do so by one-third or more of the Parties, the Depositary Governments shall convene a conference, to which they shall invite all the Parties, to consider such amendment.

2. Any amendment to this Treaty must be approved by a majority of the votes of all the Parties to this Treaty, including the votes of all of the Original Parties. The amendment shall enter into force for all Parties upon the deposit of instruments of ratification by a majority of all the Parties, including the instruments of ratification of all of the Original Parties.

ARTICLE III

1. This Treaty shall be open to all States for signature. Any State which does not sign this Treaty before its entry into force in accordance with paragraph 3 of this Article may accede to it at any time.

2. This Treaty shall be subject to ratification by signatory States. Instruments of ratification and instruments of accession shall be deposited with the Governments of the Original Parties—the United States of America, the United Kingdom of Great Britain and Northern Ireland, and the Union of Soviet Socialist Republics—which are hereby designated the Depositary Governments.

3. This Treaty shall enter into force after its ratification by all the Original Parties and the deposit of their instruments of ratification.

4. For States whose instruments of ratification or accession are deposited subsequent to the entry into force of this Treaty, it shall enter into force on the date of the deposit of their instruments of ratification or accession.

5. The Depositary Governments shall promptly inform all signatory and acceding States of the date of each signature, the date of deposit of each instrument of ratification of and accession to this Treaty, the date of its entry into force, and the date of receipt of any requests for conferences or other notices.

6. This Treaty shall be registered by the Depositary Governments pursuant to Article 102 of the Charter of the United Nations.

ARTICLE IV

This Treaty shall be of unlimited duration.

Each Party shall in exercising its national sovereignty have the right to withdraw from the Treaty if it decides that extraordinary events, related to the subject matter of this Treaty, have jeopardized the supreme interests of its country. It shall give notice of such withdrawal to all other Parties to the Treaty three months in advance.

ARTICLE V

This Treaty, of which the English and Russian texts are equally authentic, shall be deposited in the archives of the Depositary Governments. Duly certified copies of this Treaty shall be transmitted by the Depositary Governments to the Governments of the signatory and acceding States.

IN WITNESS WHEREOF the undersigned, duly authorized, have signed this Treaty.

DONE in triplicate at the city of Moscow the 5th day of August, one thousand nine hundred and sixty-three.

SELECTED BIBLIOGRAPHY ON DISARMAMENT AND OTHER RELATED QUESTIONS*

BIBLIOGRAPHIES

Focus on problems of disarmament. Feb/March 1963. 5 (2) Intercom 61-72.

Halperin, Morton H. Limited war; an essay on the development of the theory and an annotated bibliography. Cambridge, Harvard Univ., Center for International Affairs. 1962. 67p.

Selected bibliography on arms control. Harrison, Weapons System Evaluation Div., Institute for Defense Analyses. March 1962.

U. S. Air Force Academy. Library. Arms control. Feb. 1962.

U. S. Department of the Army. Library.
Disarmament: a bibliographic record, 1916-1960. Prepared for the Office of special assistant to the joint chiefs of staff for disarmament affairs. Washington. 1960.
U. S. security, arms control and disarmament 1960-61. Prepared for the Department of defense. Washington. 1961. 144pp.

U. S. Department of State. Disarmament Administration. Office of studies and projects. Research division. A basic bibliography: disarmament, arms control and national security. Washington, Gov't Print. Off. 1961. 29p. (Dep't of State pub. 7193)

Wright, Christopher. Selected critical bibliography (annotated). 1960. 89 Daedalus 1055-70.

OFFICIAL AND DOCUMENTARY SOURCES

Dean, Arthur H. The Vela program, its importance in detecting nuclear explosions and in securing an effective test ban treaty. 1961. 45 Dep't State Bull. 376-80.

Disarmament. 1961. Doc. Am. For. Relations 208-46.

Draft treaty on the discontinuance of nuclear weapons tests submitted by western delegations at Geneva conference. 1961. 44 Dep't State Bull. 870-95.

Eaton, F. M. U. S. delegation to conference on disarmament submits report to Secretary Herter, 1960. 43 Dep't State Bull. 267-74.

Exchange of messages on disarmament among heads of governments. Vienna, International Institute for Peace. 1962. 36p.

Foster, William C. The nuclear test ban issue. 1962. 48 Dep't State Bull. 398-402.

---

* Prepared under the supervision of Joseph L. Andrews, Reference Librarian of the Association.

Gehron, W. J. Geneva conference on the discontinuance of nuclear weapons tests. 1960. 43 Dep't State Bull. 482-97.

Geneva Conference on Discontinuance of Nuclear Weapons Tests. Current documents and papers. 1961. 40 Int'l Inst. for Peace. History and analysis of negotiations. 1961. Dep't State Pub. 7258.

Great Britain. Foreign Office. The search for disarmament, a summary. London, H.M.S.O. 1960. 46p.

Gromyko, Andrei A. On the negotiations in Geneva. May 30, 1962. 14 Current Dig. Soviet Press 10-13.

Gullion, Edmund A. Disarmament issues and prospects. 1961. 44 Dep't State Bull. 634-8.

Kennedy, John F. Nuclear testing and disarmament. 1962. 46 Dep't State Bull. 443-8.

Kennedy, John F. and Khrushchev, Nikita S. President Kennedy reaffirms views on framework for conduct of disarmament negotiations. 1962. 46 Dep't State Bull. 465-70.

Khrushchev, Nikita S. Disarmament is the path toward strengthening peace and ensuring friendship among peoples. 1960. 12 (2) Current Dig. Soviet Press 3-16.

Khrushchev's press conference on disarmament. 1960. 12 (23) Current Dig. Soviet Press 3-8.

Letter from Mr. Khrushchev to President Eisenhower regarding the suspension of nuclear tests and the United States proposal for an international inspection zone in the Arctic, May 9, 1958 (in Documents on international affairs, 1958. 1962. pp. 80-84)

Letter from Mr. Khrushchev to President Eisenhower regarding the suspension of nuclear tests, 22 April 1958 (in Documents on international affairs, 1958. 1962. pp. 69-76)

Lodge, Henry Cabot. The question of disarmament. 1959. 41 Dep't State Bull. 615-20.

Mr. McCloy resigns as adviser to President, reports on U.S. activities in field of disarmament and arms control. 1961. 45 Dep't State Bull. 762-70.

President Kennedy sends congress draft bill to establish U.S. disarmament agency for world peace and security. 1961. 45 Dep't State Bull. 99-106.

The problem of disarmament. 1960. Doc. Am. For. Relations 182-245.

Rusk, Dean.

Disarmament and arms control. 1962. 47 Dep't State Bull. 3-7.

U.S. outlines initial proposals of program for general and complete disarmament. 1962. 46 Dep't State Bull. 531-6.

U.S. proposes patterns for future work of disarmament conference. 1962. 46 Dep't State Bull. 618-24.

U.S. urges Soviet Union to join in ending nuclear weapons tests. 46 Dep't State Bull. 571-6.

Soviet stand on disarmament. New York, Crosscurrents Press. 1962. 150p.

Stevenson, Adlai E. Working toward a world without war. 1961. 45 Dep't State Bull. 1023-32.

A summary of developments at the conference of the 18 nation committee on disarmament, Geneva (Switzerland) March 14-June 15, 1962. 1962. 47 Dep't State Bull. 154-9.

Ten Power Disarmament Committee. Verbatim records of the meetings . . . held at the Palais des nations, Geneva, March 15-April 29, 1960 and June 7-27, 1960 . . . 1960. 940p. (Great Britain. Parliament. Cmnd. 1152)

Treaty on general and complete disarmament under strict international control; draft submitted by the USSR. 1962. 65 Am. J. Int'l L. 926-46.

United Nations. Dep't of Economic and Social Affairs. Economic and social consequences of disarmament: report of the secretary-general transmitting the study of his consultative group. 1962. 66p. (E/3593/Rev. 1)

United Nations. Disarmament Committee.

Communication dated 31 May 1962 from the co-chairmen of the conference of the eighteen nation committee on disarmament addressed to the chairman of the United Nations disarmament committee . . . 1962. v.p. (DC/203, 1962).

Official records, documents officiels, 1952 to date. New York.

Report on the proceedings of the subcommittee of the United Nations disarmament committee held at Lancaster House, London, May 13-June 22, 1954. London, H.M.S.O. 1954. 31p.

United Nations. Economic and Social Council. Economic and social consequences of disarmament: v. 2, Replies of governments and communications from international organizations. April 11, 1962. 343p. (1962. E/3593/Add. 1)

United Nations. General Assembly.

Basic provisions of a treaty on general and complete disarmament: proposals of the Soviet government submitted for consideration by the United Nations general assembly at its 15th session by N. S. Khrushchev . . . on 23 Sept. 1960. 8p. (1960. A/4505)

Declaration of the government of the Union of Soviet Socialist Republics on disarmament . . . 1960. 15p. (1960. A/4503)

Declaration of the Soviet government on general and complete disarmament. 1959. 17p. (A/4219)

United Nations. Secretariat. Historical survey of the activities of the League of Nations regarding the question of disarmament 1920-37. New York. 1951. 187p. (June 18, 1951. A/AC50/2)

United States and Soviet agree on statement of principles for disarmament negotiations: texts of two documents . . . 1961. 45 Dep't State Bull. 589-96.

United States and United Kingdom offer new proposals for banning nuclear tests. 1962. 47 Dep't State Bull. 403-16.

U. S. Arms Control and Disarmament Agency.

Arms control and disarmament (transcript of television program, state department briefing. Disarmament. First broadcast by National educational television network, Jan. 14, 1963). Washington, Gov't Print. Off. 1963. 38p.

Blueprint for the peace race; outline of basic provisions of a treaty on general and complete disarmament in a peaceful world. Washington, Gov't Print. Off. 1962. 35p.

Disarmament: the new U. S. initiative. Washington, Gov't Print. Off. 1962. 67p.

Disarmament: two approaches; a comparison: U.S. and U.S.S.R. disarmament proposals. Washington, Gov't Print. Off. 1961. 23p.

Documents on disarmament 1961. Washington, Gov't Print. Off. 1962. 798p.

Economic impacts of disarmament. Washington, Gov't Print. Off. 1962. 28p.

International negotiations on ending nuclear weapons tests. Sept. 1961-Sept. 1962. Washington, Gov't Print. Off. 1962. 333p.

Report. Washington, Gov't Print. Off. 1961-62.

Risk and security in the age of nuclear weapons. Jan. 1963. Washington, Gov't Print. Off. 1963. 17p. (Arms control pub. no. 12)

Toward a world without war; a summary of United States disarmament efforts, past and present. Washington, Gov't Print. Off. 1962. 28p.

U.S. Congress. House. Comm. on Foreign Affairs. (87.1) To establish a United States arms control agency; hearings. Washington, Gov't Print. Off. 1961. 180p.

U.S. Congress. Joint Comm. on Atomic Energy.

(86.1) Fallout from nuclear weapons tests; hearings before the special subcom. on radiation. Gov't Print. Off. 1959. 3v.

(86.2) Technical aspects of detection and inspection controls of a nuclear weapons test ban. Hearings. Gov't Print. Off. 1960. 2pts.

U.S. Congress. Senate. Comm. on Armed Forces. (87.2) Hearings before the preparedness investigating subcom. . . . on arms control and disarmament, Sept. 17-19, 1962. Washington, Gov't Print. Off. 1962. 120p.

U.S. Congress. Senate. Comm. on Foreign Relations.

(84.1) Control and reduction of armaments. Interim report . . . Gov't Print. Off. 1956. 3p.

(84.2) Control and reduction of armaments. Hearings . . . Gov't Print. Off. 1956-58. 19pts.

(86.1) Geneva test ban negotiations. Hearings . . . Gov't Print. Off. 1959. 32p.

(86.1) Testimony of John A. McCone on Geneva test ban negotiations. Hearings . . . Gov't Print. Off. 1959. 32p.

(87.1) Disarmament agency; hearings . . . Gov't Print. Off. 1961. 352p.

(87.1) United States disarmament agency report . . . Gov't Print. Off. 1961. 10p.

U.S. Congress. Senate. Comm. on Foreign Relations. Subcom. on Disarmament.

(86.1) Disarmament and foreign policy; hearings . . . Gov't Print. Off. 1959. 2pts. and periodic hearings and reports.

(86.1) Handbook on arms control and related problems in Europe; excerpts and summaries of official and unofficial proposals. Gov't Print. Off. 1959. 56p.

(86.2) Chemical-biological-radiological (CBR) warfare and its disarmament aspects; a study. Gov't Print. Off. 1960. 43p.

(86.2) Disarmament developments, spring 1960. Hearings, June 10, 1960 . . . Gov't Print. Off. 1960. 49p.

(86.2) United Nations action on disarmament: a survey of the debate of the 14th session of the general assembly . . . Gov't Print. Off. 1960. 14p.

(87.2) Renewed Geneva disarmament negotiations. July 25 and Aug. 2, 1962. Gov't Print. Off. 1963. 64p.

U.S. Department of State. Bureau of Public Affairs.
Disarmament at a glance. Washington, Gov't Print. Off. 1961. 26p. (Dep't State pub. 7058)
Disarmament; the intensified effort 1955-58. Washington, Gov't Print. Off. 1960. 66p. (General foreign policy ser. 155).

U.S. Department of State. Bureau of Public Affairs. Historical Office.
A chronology of the development of United States disarmament policy, 1953-60. Research project no. 502 . . . Washington, Gov't Print. Off. 1961. 39p.
Documents on disarmament 1945-59. 1960. 2v. (Dep't State pub. 7008)
The international control of atomic energy, growth of a policy. Summary record of the official declarations and proposals relating to the international control of atomic energy made between Aug. 6, 1945 and Oct. 15, 1946. Washington, Gov't Print. Off. 1946. 281p. (Dep't State pub. 2702)
A report on the international control of atomic energy. Washington, Gov't Print. Off. 1946. (Dep't State pub. 2498)

U.S. Library of Congress. Legislative Reference Service.
Conference on the discontinuance of nuclear weapons tests. Gov't Print. Off. 1960. 110p.
Disarmament and security; a collection of documents, 1949-55. Gov't Print. Off. 1956. 1035p.
Limitation of international traffic in arms and ammunition; excerpts from selected references chronologically arranged . . . Gov't Print. Off. 1946. 16p.

United States presents outline of a treaty on general and complete disarmament. 1962. 46 Dep't State Bull. 747-60.

United States urges prompt Soviet agreement on nuclear test ban treaty. 1961. 45 Dep't State Bull. 18-24.

Wadsworth, James J. The question of disarmament. 1960. 43 Dep't State Bull. 760-9.

Wilcox, Francis O. Disarmament; the problem and the prospects. 1960. 42 Dep't State Bull. 820-6.

BOOKS AND PAMPHLETS

Adam, R. and Judd, C. Assault at arms; a policy for disarmament. London, Weidenfeld & Nicolson. 1960. 80p.

American Academy of Arts and Sciences, Boston. Comm. on the Technical Problems of Arms Limitations.

The technical problems of arms control, by Bernard T. Feld and others. New York, Institute for International Order. 1960. 30p.

Disarmament, its politics and economics. Ed. by Seymour Melman. 1962. 398p.

Aptheker, Herbert, ed. Disarmament and the American economy, a symposium by James S. Allen and others. New York, Century Pub. 1960. 64p.

Aron, Raymond. On war. New York, Anchor Books. 1959. 143p.

Barnet, R. J. Who wants disarmament? Boston, Beacon Press. 1960. 111p.

Batten, James K. Arms control and the problem of evasion. Princeton, Center for International Studies, Woodrow Wilson School of Public & International Affairs, Princeton Univ. 1962. 28p.

Beaton, T. and Maddox, J. The spread of nuclear weapons. London, Chatto & Windus. 1962. 216p.

Bechhoefer, B. G. Postwar negotiations for arms control. Washington, Brookings Institution. 1961. 641p.

Benoit, Emile.

The economic impact of disarmament in the United States (in Melman, Seymour, ed. Disarmament: its politics and economics. American Academy of Arts & Sciences. 1962)

Economic steps towards peace (in Wright, Quincy; Evan, William M. and Deutsch, Morton, eds. Preventing world war III. New York, Simon & Schuster. 1962. pp. 136-54)

Biorklund, Elis. International atomic policy during a decade; an historical-political investigation into the problem of atomic weapons during the period 1945-55. Translated in Stockholm by Albert Read in cooperation with the author . . . London, Allen & Unwin. 1956. 148p.

Black, Cyril Wilson. A world security authority? By ten Conservative members of parliament . . . London, Conservative Political Center. 1958. 40p.

Blackett, P. M. S. Studies of war: nuclear and conventional. New York, Hill & Wang. 1962. 242p.

Bohn, Lewis C. Nonphysical techniques of disarmament inspection (in Wright, Quincy; Evan, William M. and Deutsch, Morton, eds. Preventing world war III. New York, Simon & Schuster. 1962. pp. 20-39)

Bolte, Charles Guy. The price of peace; a plan for disarmament. Boston, Beacon Press. 1956. 108p.

Bowie, Robert R. Arms control and United States foreign policy (in Henkin, Louis, ed. Arms control: issues for the public. American Assembly, Columbia Univ. Englewood Cliffs, N.J., Prentice-Hall. 1961)

Brennan, Donald G. Arms control in outer space (in American Assembly, Columbia Univ. Englewood Cliffs, N. J., Prentice-Hall. 1962. pp. 123-49)

Brennan, Donald G., ed. Arms control, disarmament and national security. New York, Braziller. 1961. 475p.

Brodie, Bernard. Strategy in the missile age. Princeton, Princeton Univ. Press. 1959. 423p.

Bull, H. The control of the arms race. New York, Praeger. 1961. 215p.

Burton, J. W. Peace theory: preconditions of disarmament. New York, Knopf. 1962. 200p.

Canada. Department of External Affairs. Report on disarmament discussions, 1957. Ottawa, E. Cloutier, Queen's Printer. 1958. 40p.

Clark, Grenville and Sohn, Louis B. World peace through world law. 2d ed. rev. Cambridge, Harvard Univ. Press. 1960. 387p.

Cockcroft, John. Problems of disarmament. London, David Davies Memorial Institute of International Studies. 1962.

Collart, Yves. Disarmament; a study guide and bibliography on the efforts of the United Nations. The Hague, Nijhoff. 1958. 110p.

Cornell Daily Sun. Problems of disarmament by Hans A. Bethe and others. New York, Monthly Review Press. 1962. 31p.

Daiches, David. Renouncing nuclear weapons (in Wright, Quincy; Evan, William M. and Deutsch, Morton, eds. Preventing world war III. New York, Simon & Schuster. 1962. pp. 62-73)

Deutsch, Morton. Reducing the reciprocal fear of surprise attack (in Wright, Quincy; Evan, William and Deutsch, Morton, eds. Preventing world war III. New York, Simon & Schuster. 1962. pp. 83-6)

Economic and social consequences of disarmament. Vienna, International Institute for Peace. 1962. 60p.

Etzioni, Amitai. The hard way to peace: a new strategy. New York, Collier Books. 1962. 285p.

Finkelstein, Laurence S. The uses of reciprocal inspection (in Melman, Seymour, ed. Disarmament: its politics and economics. American Academy of Arts & Sciences. 1962)

Finletter, Thomas K. Foreign policy: the next phase. New York, Harper, 1958. 208p.

Fisher, R. D.
Constructing rules that affect governments (in Brennan, Donald G., ed. Arms control, disarmament and national security. New York, Braziller. 1961)

Internal enforcement of international rules (in Melman, Seymour, ed. Disarmament: its politics and economics. American Academy of Arts & Sciences. 1962)

Forbes, Henry W. The strategy of disarmament. Washington, Public Affairs Press. 1962. 158p.

Frisch, D. H., ed. Arms reduction; program and issues. New York, Twentieth Century Fund. 1961. 162p.

Fromm, Erich. The case for unilateral disarmament (in Wright, Quincy; Evan, William M. and Deutsch, Morton, eds. Preventing world war III. New York, Simon & Schuster. 1962. pp. 178-91)

Frye, William R.
  Disarmament; atoms into plowshares? New York, Foreign Policy Association. 1955. 67p.
  The quest for disarmament since world war II (in Henkin, Louis, ed. Arms control: issues for the public. American Assembly, Columbia Univ. Englewood Cliffs, N. J., Prentice-Hall. 1961)

Gerard, Ralph W. Truth detection (in Wright, Quincy; Evan, William M. and Deutsch, Morton, eds. Preventing world war III. New York, Simon & Schuster. 1962. pp. 52-61)

Goetz, B.
  Progress and problems in disarmament (in Industrial relations conference, Univ. of Minnesota, 13th proceedings, 1961. pp. 50-5)
  What are the prospects for disarmament as seen in Washington (in Industrial relations conference, Univ. of Minnesota, 13th proceedings, 1961. pp. 56-61)

Goldhamer, Herbert. The political consequences of a hypothetical arms control agreement. Santa Monica, Rand Corp. 1961. 56p.

Goldwin, Robert A., ed. America armed: essays on United States military policy. Rand McNally. 1963. 140p.

Gomer, Robert. The armed arbiter (in Wright, Quincy; Evan, William M. and Deutsch, Morton, eds. Preventing world war III. New York, Simon & Schuster. 1962. pp. 74-82)

Hadley, Arthur T. The nation's safety and arms control. New York, Viking Press. 1961. 160p.

Halperin, Morton H. Arms control and inadvertent general war. Washington, Special Studies Group, Institute for Defense Analyses. 25p. (study #6)

Harrington, Charles Wilmott. The problem of disarmament in the United Nations. Geneva. 1950. 179p.

Henkin, Louis.
  Arms control and inspection in American law. With a foreword by Philip C. Jessup. New York, Columbia Univ. Press. 1958. 289p.
  The citizen's interest in the control of armaments (in Henkin, Louis, ed. Arms control: issues for the public. American Assembly, Columbia Univ. Englewood Cliffs, N. J., Prentice-Hall. 1961)

Henkin, Louis, ed. Arms control: issues for the public. American Assembly, Columbia Univ. Englewood Cliffs, N. J., Prentice-Hall. 1961. 207p.

Hughes, H. Stuart. An approach to peace and other essays. New York, Atheneum. 1962. 204p.

International Institute for Peace. General, total and controlled disarmament. Vienna. 1960. 23p.

Kelman, Herbert C. Internationalizing military force (in Wright, Quincy; Evan, William M. and Deutsch, Morton, eds. Preventing world war III. New York, Simon & Schuster. 1962. pp. 106-22)

Kent, Glenn A. On the interaction of opposing forces under possible arms agreements. Cambridge, Center for International Affairs, Harvard Univ. 1963. 40p.

Keyston, J. E. The nature of the disarmament problem. Toronto, Canadian Institute of International Affairs. 1961. 24p.

King, James E., Jr. Arms control and United States security (in Henkin, Louis, ed. Arms control: issues for the public. American Assembly, Columbia Univ. Englewood Cliffs, N. J., Prentice-Hall. 1961. pp. 76-111)

Lapp, Ralph E. Kill and overkill. New York, Basic Books. 1962. 197p.

Larson, Arthur. Arms control through world law (in Brennan, Donald G., ed. Arms control, disarmament and national security. New York, Braziller. 1961)

Lefever, Ernest W., ed. Arms and arms control: a symposium. New York, Praeger. 1962. 334p.

Liddell Hart, B. H. Deterrent or defense: a fresh look at the west's military position. New York, Praeger. 1960. 257p.

Luard, Evan. Peace and opinion. London and New York, Oxford Univ. Press. 1962. 170p.

Martin, Andrews. Collective security, a progress report. Paris, UNESCO. 1952. 243p.

Marzani, C. and Perlo, V. Dollars and sense of disarmament. New York, Marzani & Munsell. 1960. 240p.

Mackintosh and Willetts. Arms control and the Soviet interest (in Henkin, Louis, ed. Arms control: issues for the public. American Assembly, Columbia Univ. Englewood Cliffs, N. J., Prentice-Hall. 1961)

McNaughton, John T. Arms restraint in military decisions (speech). Ann Arbor, International Arms Control Symposium, Univ. of Michigan. Dec. 19, 1962. 19p.

Melman, Seymour, ed. Disarmament: its politics and economics. American Academy of Arts and Sciences. 1962.

Melman, Seymour.

Inspection by the people (in Wright, Quincy; Evan, William M. and Deutsch, Morton, eds. Preventing world war III. New York, Simon & Schuster. 1962. pp. 40-51)

Inspection for disarmament. New York, Columbia Univ. Press. 1958. 291p.

The peace race. New York, Braziller. 1962. 152p.

Mezerik, Avraham G., ed.

Atom tests and radiation hazards; test ban efforts, U.N. cold war conferences, chronology. New York, International Review Service. 1961. (V.7, no. 68)

Disarmament: impact on underdeveloped countries, political,

social, economic. New York, International Review Service. 1961. 41p.

New proposals for disarmament, including Khrushchev, U.N. 10 nation group. New York, International Review Service. 1959. 51p.

Millard, Everett. Freedom in a federal world. 2d ed. rev. New York, Oceana. 1960.

Millis, Walter. The uselesness of military power (in Goldwin, Robert A., ed. America armed: essays on United States military policy. Rand McNally. 1963)

Moch, Jules Salvador. Human folly: to disarm or perish? Trans. by Edward Huans with an introduction by Albert Einstein. London, Gollancz. 1955. 222p.

Morgenthau, Hans J. Politics among nations. New York, Knopf. 1954. 600p.

Morley, Lorna. Nuclear test ban. May 13, 1958. Editorial Research Reports. 16p.

Morray, Joseph P. From Yalta to disarmament; cold war debate. New York, Monthly Review Press. 1961. 368p.

Moskowitz, Harry and Roberts, Jack. U.S. security, arms control and disarmament, 1960-61. Washington, U.S. Army Library. 1961. 144p.

Murray, Thomas E. Nuclear policy for war and peace. Cleveland, World Pub. 1960. 241p.

Naess, Arne. Nonmilitary defense (in Wright, Quincy; Evan, William M. and Deutsch, Morton, eds. Preventing world war III. New York, Simon & Schuster. 1962. pp. 123-35)

National Planning Association. Special Project Comm. on Security through Arms Control. Strengthening the government for arms control; a report. Washington, Gov't Print. Off. 1960. 27p.

Noel-Baker, Philip John. The arms race; a programme for world disarmament. London, Stevens. 1958. 579p.

Nogee, J. L. Soviet policy towards international control of atomic energy. Notre Dame, Univ. of Notre Dame Press. 1961. 306p.

Nutting, Anthony. Disarmament: an outline of the negotiations. New York, Oxford Univ. Press. 1959. 68p.

Osgood, Charles. The uses of military power in the cold war (in Goldwin, Robert A., ed. America armed: essays on United States military policy. Rand McNally. 1963)

Piotrow, P. T. Arms control: 1958. Editorial Research Reports. 1958. 16p.

The present stage of the talks on general and complete disarmament. Vienna, International Institute for Peace. 1961. 29p.

Preston, Richard A. Can we disarm? Jan. 1958. Behind the Headlines (Canadian Inst. of Int'l Affairs) 16p.

Rapacki, A. Peaceful coexistence and disarmament. 1961. 40 Current Articles, Interviews & Statements on Disarmament. 11p.

Read, Thornton. A proposal to neutralize nuclear weapons. Princeton, Center of International Studies, Woodrow Wilson School of Public & International Affairs, Princeton Univ. 1961. 50p.

Russell, Bertrand, 3d Earl. Has man a future? New York, Simon & Schuster. 1962. 128p.

Schelling, T. C.
A special surveillance force (in Wright, Quincy; Evan, William and Deutsch, Morton, eds. Preventing world war III. New York, Simon & Schuster. 1962. pp. 87-105)
Surprise attack and disarmament. Santa Monica, Rand Corp. 1958. 48p.

Schelling, T. C. and Halperin, M. H. Strategy and arms control. New York, Twentieth Century Fund. 1961. 148p.

Singer, J. David. Deterrence, arms control and disarmament. Columbus, Ohio State Univ. Press. 1962. 279p.

Singer, J. David, ed. Weapons management in world politics. Proceedings of the international arms control symposium held in Ann Arbor, Dec. 17-20, 1962. 1963. 7 (3) J. Conflict Resolution; 1 (4) J. Arms Control (combined in one issue)

Slessor, John. The great deterrent. New York, Praeger. 1957. 321p.

Slick, Tom. Permanent peace; a check and balance plan. Englewood Cliffs, N. J., Prentice-Hall. 1958. 181p.

Sohn, Louis B. Adjudication and enforcement in arms control (in Brennan, Donald G., ed. Arms control, disarmament and national security. New York, Braziller. 1961)

Soviet News. Disarmament, the road to a world without war. London, Soviet Booklets. 1962. 123p.

Spanier, J. W. and Nogee, J. L. The politics of disarmament: a study in Soviet-American gamesmanship. New York, Praeger. 1962. 226p.

Spingarn, Jerome H. Is disarmament possible? New York, Public Affairs Committee. 1956. 28p.

Stanford, Neal. What is the score on nuclear tests? June 15, 1959. For. Pol. Bull.

Stillman, Edmund O. and Pfaff, William. The new politics; America and the end of the postwar world. New York, Coward, McCann. 1961. 191p.

Strachey, John. On the prevention of war. New York, St. Martin's Press. 1963. 334p.

Tatum, L. B. An examination of Soviet disarmament policy with emphasis upon principles of disarmament revealed therein. Ann Arbor, University Microfilms. 1962. 759p. (Thesis, Syracuse Univ. Graduate School. 1961)

Teller, Ludwig. The case for continuing nuclear tests. Jan/Feb. 1961. Headline Series, Foreign Policy Association.

Thomas, Hugh. Disarmament—the way ahead. Foreword by Kenneth Younger. London, Fabian International Bureau. 1957. 33p.

Wadsworth, James J. The price of peace. New York, Praeger. 1962. 127p.

Warburg, J. P. Disarmament: the challenge of the nineteen sixties. Garden City, N. Y., Doubleday. 1961. 288p.

Waskow, Arthur I. The limits of defense. Garden City, N. Y., Doubleday. 1962. 119p.

Wilson, Hugh Robert. Disarmament and the cold war in the thirties. 1st ed. New York, Vantage Press. 1963. 87p.

Woods Hole Summer Study. Verification and response in disarmament agreements, summary report and two annex volumes. Institute for Defense Analyses under contract with the United States Arms Control & Disarmament Agency. 1962.

Wright, Quincy; Evan, William M. and Deutsch, Morton. Preventing world war III; some proposals. New York, Simon & Schuster. 1962. 460p.

Young, R. W. The aerial inspection plan and air space sovereignty (in U.S. Library of Congress, Legislative reference service. Legal problems of space exploration: a symposium. Washington. 1961. pp. 46-64)

Younger, Kenneth Gilmour. Diplomacy in the age of nuclear strategy. Nottingham, Eng. 1961. 16p. (Montague Burton international relations lecture 1960-61)

PERIODICAL REFERENCES

Andreyev, G. Disarmament talks: truth and fiction. 1961. 7 (6) Int'l Aff. (Moscow) 3-14.

Barnet, Richard J. The Soviet attitude on disarmament. 1961. 10 Prob. of Communism 32-7.

Bartos, Milan. Legal aspects of disarmament. 1960. 11 Rev. Int'l Aff. 8-10.

Bechhoefer, B. G. The disarmament deadlock: 1946-1955. 1962. 42 Current Hist. 257-66.

Benoit, Emile.
Affording disarmament; an analysis, a model, some proposals. 1962. 5 Colum. U. Forum 4-10.
Economics of disarmament. 1962. 6 Marq. Bus. Rev. 16-21.

Berc, H. T. Achieving disarmament through review of the U.N. charter. 1955. 36 Chi. B. Rec. 425-7.

Bloomfield, L. P. Arms control and world government. 1962. 14 World Politics 633-45.

Bogdanov, O. Disarmament in the light of international law. 1958. Soviet Yb. Int'l L. 93-127.

Bonsal, Dudley B. Lawyer's role in the search for peace. 1961. 16 Record 313-25.

Brown, S. Invulnerable retaliatory capability and arms control. 1961. 13 World Politics 528-43.

Buchan, Alastair. Deterrent and disarmament. 1962. 42 Military Rev. 73-86.

Chamberlin, William H. Disarmament: hope or trap? the danger of words for our weapons. 1961. 5 Modern Age 231-7.

Clark, J. S. The influence of congress in the formulation of disarmament policy. 1962. 342 Annals 147-53.

Croy, Robert H., jr. International inspection: from proposal to realization. 1959. 13 Int'l Org. 495-504.

De Weerd, Harvey A. Arms control and the legacy of the past. 1962. 18 Bull. Atomic Scientists 18-28.

Disarmament. 1959. Current Notes Int'l Aff. 597-604.

Disarmament and nuclear policy. March 1962. 1 Can. Inst. Int'l Aff. Mo. Rep. 21-32.

Disarmament and nuclear testing. 1962. 33 Current Notes Int'l Aff. 5-15.

Disarmament and related questions. 1960. U. N. Yb. 3-29.

Disarmament: a panel. Enforcement of disarmament: the problem of the response (R. D. Fisher: comments, R. A. Falk, J. T. McNaughton; R. J. Barnet, discussion). 1962. 56 Am. Soc'y Int'l L. Proc. 1-18.

Disarmament—comparison of Soviet and Western proposals. 1960. 16 Bull. Atomic Scientists 336-9.

Disarmament negotiations 1960-61. July 1961. Current Notes Int'l Aff. 5-14.

Dougherty, James E. The disarmament debate: a review of current literature; disarmament with inspection. 1961/62. 5 Orbis 342-59.

Dutt, R. P. British labour movement and nuclear disarmament. 1960. 6 (12) Int'l Aff. (Moscow) 51-7.

Experts report on economics of a disarmed world. 1962. 9 U.N. Rev. 22-4.

Ferguson, A. R. Mechanics of some limited disarmament measures. 1961. 51 Am. Econ. Rev., Pap. & Proc. 479-88.

Finkelstein, Lawrence S.
Arms inspection. Nov. 1962. 540 Int'l Conciliation 5-89.
The United Nations and organizations for the control of armaments. 1962. 16 Int'l Org. 1-19.

Fisher, R. D. Enforcement of disarmament: the problem of the response. 1962. 56 Am. Soc'y Int'l L. Proc. 1-17.

Fliess, P. J. The legality of atmospheric nuclear tests. 1962. 15 U. Fla. L. Rev. 21-32.

Foster, W. C. Arms control and disarmament in a divided world. 1962. 342 Annals 80-8.

Freeman, Harrop A. and Yaker, Stanley. Disarmament and atomic control: legal and non-legal problems. 1957. 43 Cornell L. Q. 236-62.

Frye, William R. K's disarmament plan: pie-in-sky? Oct. 15, 1959. For. Pol. Bull.

Galay, Nikolai. The duplicity of Soviet Disarmament policy. 1961/62. 31 Soviet Aff. Analysis Serv. 1-5.

Green, Howard C. The United Nations and disarmament. 1960. 12 External Aff. (Can.) 830-46.

Gromov, L. Some economic aspects of disarmament. 1960. 6 (3) Int'l Aff. (Moscow) 26-34.

Gross, E. A. Major problems in disarmament. 1956. 51 Nw. U. L. Rev. 299-309.

91

Hammond, P. Y. Some difficulties of self-enforcing arms agreements. 1962. 6 J. Conflict Resolution 103-15.

Henkin, Louis. Arms inspection and the constitution. May 1959. 15 Bull. Atomic Scientists 6; 1960. 11 Hastings L. J. 267-84.

Horowitz, Irving L. Arms, policies and games. 1961/62. 31 Am. Scholar 94-107.

Howard, Michael. Limited armament zones in Europe. 1962. 17 Bull. Atomic Scientists 9-14.

Iklé, Fred C. After detection—what? 1961. 39 For. Aff. 208-20.

Jacob, Philip E. The disarmament consensus: toward balance and phased disarmament; the problem of control. 1960. 14 Int'l Org. 233-60.

Kelly, George A. Arms control and the military establishment. 1961. 41 Military Rev. 62-72.

Khvostov, V. Disarmament negotiations. 1961. 7 (2) Int'l Aff. (Moscow) 60-7.

Kissinger, Henry A. Arms control, inspection and surprise attack. 1960. 38 For. Aff. 557-75.

Kumar, M. Recent advances in research on disarmament. 1962. 3 Int'l Studies 335-48.

Lahoda, T. The disarmament problem and the ten nation committee. 1960. 7 Rev. Contemp. L. 311-25.

Levine, Robert A.
Breaking the arms stalemate. 1962. 18 Bull Atomic Scientists 8-11.
Disarmament and arms control. 1962. 45 New Leader 15-18.
Facts and morals in the arms debate. 1962. 14 World Politics 239-58.

Lombardi, Ricardo. Disarmament and the American economy. 1960. 11 Rev. Int'l Aff. 10-12.

McCloy, John J. Balance sheet on disarmament. 1962. 40 For. Aff. 339-59.

Martin, L. W. Political settlements and arms control. 1962. 42 Current Hist. 296-301.

Memorandum on disarmament. 1961. 8 Rev. Contemp. L. 128-36.

Menzies, D.
Disarmament. 1961. 32 (10) Current Notes Int'l Aff. 23-31.
Soviet resumption of nuclear tests. 1961. 32 (9) Current Notes Int'l Aff. 32-7.

Murray, Thomas E. Ending an era of terror. 1960. 16 Bull. Atomic Scientists 162-6.

Nanes, A. S. Disarmament in the last seven years. 1962. 42 Current Hist. 267-74.

Noel-Baker, Philip. Disarmament 1959. 1960. 15 World Aff. (N. Z.) 19-22.

Nogee, Joseph. The diplomacy of disarmament. 1960. 526 Int'l Conciliation 235-303.

Nutting, Anthony. Disarmament, Europe and security. 1960. 36 Int'l Aff. (London) 1-16.

Orear, Jay. A new approach to inspection. 1961. 17 Bull. Atomic Scientists 107-10.

Our ideas of a world without arms. 1962. 8 (7) Int'l Aff. (Moscow) 49-64.

Outline of basic provisions of a treaty on general and complete disarmament in a peaceful world, submitted by the United States delegation to the U.N. committee on disarmament. Geneva, April 18, 1962. 1962. 56 Am. J. Int'l L. 899-925.

Pechota, V. The disarmament question before the fifteenth session of the U.N. general assembly. 1960. 7 (2) Rev. Contemp. L. 126-34.

Perkins, Dexter. Peace and armament. 1960. 36 Va. L. Rev. 497-516.

Piel, Gerard. The economics of disarmament. 1960. 16 Bull. Atomic Scientists 117-22.

Polanyi, John C. Armaments policies for the sixties. 1961. 17 Bull. Atomic Scientists 403-6.

Present problems and prospects of disarmament (in Interparliamentary union, 49th conference, Tokyo, 1960. Compte rendu. Genève. 1961. pp. 468-88, 869-990, 1097-8)

Rabinowitch, E. et al. Arms control and disarmament. 1961. 17 Bull. Atomic Scientists 123-53.

Rapacki, Adam. The Polish plan for a nuclear-free zone today. 1963. 39 Int'l Aff. (London) 1-12.

Resumption of nuclear testing. 1961. 32 (9) Current Notes Int'l Aff. 10-25.

Rhyne, Charles S.
Law for weapons. 1958. 26 Tenn. L. Rev. 1-8.
Lawyer's part in plans for peace and disarmament. 1955. 22 J. B. A. D. C. 401-9.

Russell, Bertrand, 3d Earl. The case for British nuclear disarmament. 1962. 17 Bull. Atomic Scientists 6-10.

Schelling, T. C.
Arms control; proposal for a special surveillance force. 1960. 13 World Politics 1-18.
Arms control will not cut down defense costs. 39 Harv. Bus. Rev. 6-14.
The role of deterrence in total disarmament. 1962. 40 For. Aff. 392-406.

Scott, R. A ban on nuclear tests. 1962. 38 Int'l Aff. (London) 501-10.

Singer, J. David. From deterrence to disarmament. 1961. 17 Int'l J. 307-26.

Sokol, Anthony E. Disarmament—is it possible? 1961. 87 U.S. Naval Inst. Proc. 56-64.

Speidel, H. The truth about the disarmament talks. 1960. 17 Fifteen Nations 10-19.

The suspension of nuclear tests. 1962. 33 (9) Current Notes Int'l Aff. 32-44.

Szilard, Leo. Are we on the road to war? 1962. 18 Bull. Atomic Scientists 23-30.

Taubenfeld, H. J. Nuclear testing and international law. 1962. 16 Sw. L. J. 365.

Thompson, Carol T. A history of disarmament proposals. 1959. 36 Current Hist. 38-41.

The United Nations and disarmament. 1960. 12 (11) External Aff. 830-46.

Varela, A. Latin America and the need for disarmament. 1960. Int'l Inst. for Peace, 33 Current Articles, Interviews & Statements 1-7.

Various draft resolutions on the disarmament question submitted to the 15th session of the U.N. general assembly. Vienna, International Institute for Peace. 1961. 23p.

Vavra, S. The problem of general and complete disarmament following the XVth session of the general assembly of the United Nations. 1961. 8 Rev. Contemp. L. 137-44.

Vreeden, D. C. Buurman van. The armaments control agency of the western European union. 1960. 15 Fifteen Nations 62-5.

Wadsworth, James J. The quest for disarmament. 1961. 44 New Leader 5-6.

Wilcox, Francis O. Disarmament—the problem and prospects. 1960. 54 Am. Soc'y Int'l L. Proc. 38-47.

Wilson, E. R. Disarmament and the cold war (in Industrial relations, conference, Univ. of Minnesota, 13th proceedings. Minneapolis. 1961. 62-70)

Young, Wayland and Young, Elizabeth. Disarmament vs. arms control; a discussion of criteria. 1961. 32 Commentary 124-34.

NOTES
to
WORKING PAPER

[1] 33 Department of State Bulletin 171 (1955).

[2] U.N. Disarmament Commission, Subcommittee of the Disarmament Commission, Fourth Report, Doc. DC/SC.1/PV.88 (March 19, 1957) pp. 21-30, quoted and discussed in Bechhoefer, *Post-War Negotiations for Arms Control* (1961) Chapter XIV.

[3] See, *e.g.*, discussion in Etzioni, *The Hard Way to Peace* (1962) Chapter 5; Barnet, "The Soviet Attitude on Disarmament," in *Problems of Communism*, May-June 1961 p. 32.

[4] See, *e.g.*, King, "Arms Control and United States Security," in *Arms Control: Issues for the Public* (Henkin ed.) 1961; Schelling and Halperin, *Strategy and Arms Control* (1961), pp. 1-6.

[5] Most recently in Blueprint for the Peace Race, Outline of Basic Provisions of a Treaty on General and Complete Disarmament in a Peaceful World, April 18, 1962 (U.S. Arms Control and Disarmament Agency Publication 4).

[6] *E.g.*, Schelling and Halperin, *Strategy and Arms Control* (1961) Chapter 8.

[7] See Henkin, "The Citizen's Interest in the Control of Armaments," in *Arms Control: Issues for the Public* (Henkin ed.) 1961. For a good examination of the issues of disarmament see Bull, *The Control of the Arms Race* (1961).

[8] See Bowie, "Arms Control and United States Foreign Policy" in *Arms Control: Issues for the Public* (Henkin ed.) 1961.

[9] See Mackintosh and Willetts, "Arms Control and the Soviet Interest," in *Arms Control: Issues for the Public* (Henkin ed.) 1961. See also Barnet, *supra* note 3, and Barnet, *Who Wants Disarmament* (1960) Part II.

[10] Some of these may fall within the "gamesmanship" of disarmament. Compare Spanier and Nogee, *The Politics of Disarmament* (1962) Chapter II.

[11] See, for example, Stillman and Pfaff, *The New Politics: America and the End of the Postwar World* (1961).

[12] See Brodie, *Strategy in the Missile Age* (1959). See also Bull, *supra* note 7, Chapter 2; King, *supra* note 4; for a more popular presentation see Hadley, *The Nation's Safety and Arms Control* (1961) Chapter 2.

[13] An estimate of present Soviet and U.S. capabilities appears below, accompanying note 29.

[14] See Bowie, *supra* note 8.

[15] The fullest history of post-war negotiations is in Bechhoefer, *supra* note 2. See also Collart, *Disarmament: a Study Guide and Bibliography on the Efforts of the United Nations* (1958). For a summary version, see Frye, "The Quest for Disarmament since World War II," in *Arms Control: Issues for the Public* (Henkin ed.) 1961.

[16] See Spanier and Nogee, *The Politics of Disarmament* (1962), 5-6, and *passim;* compare Nutting, *Disarmament, an Outline of the Negotiations* (1959): "I cannot honestly say that I believe there was ever a moment in all these negotiations when a real agreement was a practical possibility." Compare also Mackintosh and Willetts, *supra* note 9.

[17] The so-called "Baruch Plan" was based on the Acheson-Lilienthal report, "A Report on the International Control of Atomic Energy," U.S. Department of State Publication No. 2498 (1946). See also "International Control of Atomic Energy," U.S. Department of State Publication No. 2702 (1946).

[18] Compare Nutting, *supra* note 16; also Bechhoefer, *supra* note 2, 365-70, 386-90, 399-413.

[19] "Declaration of the Soviet Government on General and Complete Disarmament" U.N. Doc.A/4219 (Sept. 19, 1959). The Soviet Union later presented a draft treaty to the Eighteen Nation Committee on Disarmament (ENDC/2, 15 March 1962).

[20] The West made numerous statements in reaction to the Soviet proposal (see Bechhoefer, *supra* note 2, 531-57). Then, after the Declaration to the General Assembly by President Kennedy on September 25, 1961, the United States, on April 18, 1962, submitted to the Eighteen Nation Disarmament Committee an expanded "Outline of Basic Provisions of a Treaty on General and Complete Disarmament in a Peaceful World." See *Blueprint for the Peace Race,* U.S. Arms Control and Disarmament Agency Publication 4.

[21] *Id.,* Stage 1.

[22] *E.g.,* Teller, "The Case for Continuing Nuclear Tests," *Headline Series (Foreign Policy Association—World Affairs Council)* January-February, 1961. Compare his statement in *Arms and Arms Control* (Lefever ed.) (1962) p. 279. See note 55.

[23] President Kennedy and Prime Minister Macmillan made this offer on September 3, 1961; Premier Khrushchev rejected it on September 9.

[24] On December 19, 1962, Premier Khrushchev in a letter to President Kennedy accepted the principle of "on-site" inspection and offered "two-or-three" international inspections a year on Soviet territory. Negotiations following this letter left the parties too far apart on the minimum number of on-site inspections.

[25] See note 17 above.

[26] This, in effect, is the position taken by the United States in the McCloy-Zorin talks, in the declaration of September 1961, and in its draft treaty proposal of April 18, 1962. See note 20 above.

[27] Compare Osgood, "The Uses of Military Power in the Cold War," with Millis, "The Uselessness of Military Power," in *America*

Armed: Essays on United States Military Policy (Goldwin ed.) (1963), pp. 1, 22.

[28] See the discussion of the prospects for disarmament below.

[29] In particular, see an unclassified exposition of East-West strength "The Communist Bloc and the Western Alliances, the Military Balance," now published annually by the Institute for Strategic Studies, London.

[30] See, *e.g., Verification and Responses in Disarmament Agreements*, Annex Volume 1, Appendix D, Woods Hole Summer Study (1962).

[31] Compare the discussion in King, *supra* note 4.

[32] *E.g., Verification and Response in Disarmament Agreements*, Annex Volume 1, Part II, Woods Hole Summer Study (1962); see also the Summary Report of that study.

[33] See *id.*, particularly the Summary Report, and Annex Volume II.

[34] See, *e.g.*, Fisher, "Constructing Rules that Affect Governments," in *Arms Control, Disarmament, and National Security* (Brennan ed.) 1961; Fisher, "Internal Enforcement of International Rules," in *Disarmament: Its Politics and Economics* (Melman ed.) 1962. Compare Sohn, "Adjudication and Enforcement in Arms Control," and Larson, "Arms Control through World Law" in *Arms Control, Disarmament, and National Security, supra.*
See also the Woods Hole Summer Study, *supra* note 32, Annex Volume II.

[35] *Id.*, Summary Report pp. 8 *et seq.*, and Annex Volume II.

[36] *Id.*, Annex Volume I, Part II.

[37] *Id.*, Summary Report and Annex Volume II. See also Finkelstein, "The Uses of Reciprocal Inspection" in *Disarmament: Its Politics and Economics* (Melman ed.) 1962.

[38] This was the U.S. position for all stages of disarmament in its proposal of April 18, 1962, *supra* note 20. There are indications that the United States is now considering reciprocal inspection for early stages.

[39] *Ibid.*

[40] The most thorough public consideration of the problems of response, their relation to the substantive provisions of an agreement, and to the verification arrangements, is in the Woods Hole Summer Study of 1962, "Verification and Response in Disarmament Agreements," Summary Report and two Annex Volumes.

[41] Recall the ineffective attempts to maintain sanctions against Italy after its aggression against Ethiopia in 1935.

[42] The United States proposal of April 18, 1962, *supra* note 20, contemplates that with progressive disarmament the parties will also strengthen rules of international conduct and machinery for the peaceful settlement of disputes.

[43] For a carefully wrought optimal solution, see Clark and Sohn, *"World Peace through World Law"* (2d ed. 1960). See also Larson, *supra* note 34.

[44] See note 26 above.

[45] See notes 40 and 43 above.

[46] See note 42 above.

[47] For a comprehensive study of the questions raised here, and others, see Henkin, *Arms Control and Inspection in American Law* (1958). Summary articles on the subject may be found in Henkin, *Arms Inspection and the Constitution,* Bulletin of the Atomic Scientists, May 1959, and, in a larger version, in 11 Hastings L.J. 267 (1960). See also Freeman and Yaker, *Disarmament and Atomic Control: Legal and Non-Legal Aspects,* 43 Cornell L.Q. 236 (1957).

[48] Henkin, *supra* note 47, pp. 39-45.

[49] Mr. Justice Frankfurter, in *Sweezy* v. *New Hampshire,* 354 U.S. 234, 255, 262 (1957).

[50] Since consideration of this question in the 1958 study, *supra* note 47 pp. 64-83, the Supreme Court decided *Frank* v. *Maryland,* 359 U.S. 360 (1959), upholding the right of a Maryland health inspector to enter a dwelling without a warrant.

[51] Henkin, *supra* note 47, Chapter V.

[52] See, *e.g.*, Economic Impacts of Disarmament, a Report of the Panel on Economic Impacts of Disarmament submitted to the United States Arms Control and Disarmament Agency, January 1962; Benoit, "The Economic Impact of Disarmament in the United States" in *Disarmament: Its Politics and Economics* (Melman ed.) 1962.

[53] Compare Schelling, "Arms Control Will Not Cut Defense Cost," in *Harvard Business Review,* March-April 1961.

[54] For a fuller exposition of these views, see Henkin, "The Citizen's Interest in Arms Control" in *Arms Control: Issues for the Public* (Henkin ed.) 1961.

[55] Compare, *e.g.*, Bethe, "The Case for Ending Nuclear Tests," with Teller, "The Case for Continuing Nuclear Tests," in *Headline Series (Foreign Policy Association—World Affairs Center)* 1961, reproduced in part in *Arms and Arms Control* (Lefever ed.) 1962.

[56] See, for example, the exchanges between Senator Dodd of Connecticut and Adrian S. Fisher, Deputy Director of the United States Arms Control and Disarmament Agency, in the Washington Post, March 1, 1963, page A-14, March 4, page A-16, March 7, page A-26. See also the letters of Mr. James Newman on March 9, page A-8 and of Representative Hosmer on March 13, page A-16.

[57] See the discussion of inspection above, beginning at text accompanying note 35.

91333

341.67
H224